ESSAYS BY DIVERS HANDS

being the transactions of
the Royal Society of Literature
New Series: Volume XLVI

EDITED BY RALEIGH TREVELYAN, FRSL

The Boydell Press

The Royal Society of Literature

First published 1990 by The Boydell Press, Woodbridge

The Boydell Press is an imprint of Boydell & Brewer Ltd
PO Box 9, Woodbridge, Suffolk IP12 3DF
and of Boydell & Brewer Inc.
PO Box 41026, Rochester, NY 14604, USA

A Royal Society of Literature publication

ISBN 0 85115 277 5

ISSN 0261–216x

British Library Cataloguing in Publication Data
Essays by divers hands: being the
    transactions of the Royal Society of Literature.
    1. English literature—Critical studies—
    Serials
    820.9
    ISBN 0-85115-277-5

This publication is printed on acid-free paper

Photoset by Rowland Phototypesetting Ltd
Bury St Edmunds, Suffolk
Printed and bound in Great Britain by
St Edmundsbury Press Ltd, Bury St Edmunds, Suffolk

ESSAYS BY DIVERS HANDS:

BEING THE TRANSACTIONS OF THE
ROYAL SOCIETY OF LITERATURE

New Series: Volume XLVI

CONTENTS

NOTES ON MEMORIAL LECTURES

Joseph Bard   Founded in 1978 by Eileen Agar, widow of Joseph Bard, in memory of her husband who was a Fellow of the Society and member of Council from 1946 to 1975.

Joyce Brown   To honour the memory of Joyce Brown who was a member and benefactor of the Society.

Willard Connely   Founded in 1968 to provide a lecture every third year on American literature or an American author.

Don Carlos Coloma   Founded in 1964 in the will of Miss Olga Turner to perpetuate the memory of Don Carlos Coloma, Spanish author.

Giff Edmonds   Founded in 1939 by Miss Sophia Edmonds in memory of her brother, Lieutenant Gifford Edmonds, who was killed at Magersfontein in 1899.

Stephen Graham   Founded in 1980 with a bequest by Mrs Vera Graham in memory of her husband, Stephen Graham, who was a Fellow of the Society for twenty-five years.

Marie Stopes   Founded in 1968 in memory of Marie Stopes, Fellow and benefactor of the Society.

Katya Reissner   Founded by Alexander Reissner, a member of the Society, in memory of his mother who was a musician and lover of literature.

Tredegar   Founded in 1936 by the 2nd Viscount Tredegar in memory of his father.

Wedmore   Founded in 1944 by Miss Millicent Wedmore in memory of her father, Sir Frederick Wedmore.

INTRODUCTION

SOME years ago a previous editor in this series, John Guest, remarked that *Divers Hands* gave a hint of subaqueous activity, diving for pearls he thought. *The Oxford English Dictionary* puts arch. or joc. in brackets after the word 'divers'. So perhaps this now long-established title, arch. rather than joc., is not only excusable but appropriate for a society founded in 1825.

I shall have to admit that my editorial job has not been all that exacting, as all the essays printed here are by respected and distinguished writers and scholars. The problem has been more one of selection, from lectures read to the Society over two years or so, bearing in mind the length of the book and the fact that some of the speakers might have been friends of long standing. However the task was made easier when I discovered that some of the lectures had been delivered from notes only, never intended to be read. I also decided to omit essays which could be classed as of topical interest, and thus of less relevance to readers who might wish to turn to this book in decades to come.

For the record, therefore, I should like to mention three of these omissions, which were all very enjoyable to hear. One was the address by the Minister of the Arts, the Right Honorable Richard Luce MP on his policy regarding literature. The others were *Does Literature Need Readers?* by Martyn Goff, at the time Chairman of the National Book League, and *A Note from an Immortal Bibliophile* by Tom Rosenthal, the leading London publisher.

The titles of these lectures, added to those printed in the book, do at least show the considerable, indeed—to make a horrid pun—diverse, range of subjects that might be covered in a single year. Nevertheless I have had cause recently to look through volumes in the series over the past fifty years, and it is interesting—though not surprising

—to find that Shakespeare and Jane Austen have been favourite subjects. In this volume essays on both appear, but presented with particular originality and indeed wit. Leon Garfield modestly compares his problem of turning the plays of Shakespeare into stories with playing Beethoven's Ninth Symphony on a penny whistle. One can indeed appreciate the difficulties of conveying the richness of Shakespearean language in simple narrative, but at least he has not had the constraints of Dr Bowdler and his sister, or of Constance Maxwell in her Juvenile Edition of 1828 when faced with the events in Imogen's bedchamber in *Cymbeline*. He concentrates mainly on the task—and sometimes the dilemmas—when retelling *Julius Caesar*, and his enjoyment during this 'pilgrimage' is obvious, a pleasure to read.

There is, as Gilbert Phelps says, a popular image of Jane Austen merely as a witty social satirist of a 'realistic' kind. But he has sought what he calls a distinction of emphases, away from conventional realism, and he even at one stage thought of calling his lecture 'Surrealist Elements in Jane Austen's Fiction'. Throughout her books Jane Austen is concerned with her heroine's inner progress from illusion to reality, and in so doing uses symbolism, allegory and various conceits which Dr Phelps delightfully illustrates. He picks out three prime 'surrealist' episodes, two being in *Mansfield Park*, the expedition to Sotherton and the theatricals, and the other the sequence at Box Hill in *Emma*. Poetry and the Victorian novelists, again perhaps not surprisingly, have also been recurrent themes of lectures in past years, by Binyon, Houseman, Drinkwater, Sackville-West, de la Mare . . . The list is very long. In this volume poetry is represented by P. J. Kavanagh on Ivor Gurney whose reputation has of course been steadily growing, particularly since P. J. Kavanagh himself edited the *Collected Poems* in 1982. Gurney's life was sad and unsettled which makes his 'love poem to the world', the 'old absolutes', all the more moving.

The Society is in fact contemplating republishing at some future date a collection in one volume of past essays on Victorian novelists. Even if *Almayer's Folly* appeared in 1895 and *The Nigger of the Narcissus* in 1897 in no sense could John Halperin on *Conrad Alone* be considered eligible in that eventuality. His essay is an absorbing character sketch, showing how the novels grew out of life and experience; out of solitude, wanderings and exile. Conrad only arrived, amazingly, in England when he was aged twenty, but as Edith

Wharton remarked he came to worship England like a lover. Another solitary but completely different character, Giuseppe Tomasi di Lampedusa, also had a passion for the English language and more especially for English literature, and indeed for French literature. Quoting E. M. Forster this time, *The Leopard* is one of the 'great lonely books', a posthumous masterpiece that could even have been unfinished. In contrast to Conrad, Lampedusa led a mostly uneventful life, against an aristocratic background, and it is a tribute to David Gilmour's skill as a biographer and researcher that he has produced such a masterly account.

Dr Vivian Green's lecture was to celebrate the 500th anniversary of the birth of Cranmer, one of the major contributors to the development of the English language. Cranmer died a martyr, but he 'presided over a church in transition, revising services, reformulating doctrine and re-drafting laws, creating a single, comprehensive church which was moderate, without papalism, but in many ways intrinsically Catholic'. The break with Rome meant the introduction of English as a medium of worship. As a result, as Dr Green says, Cranmer's Book of Common Prayer has become part of our literary unconscious to be set side by side with the Authorized Version of the Bible. The Society's Honorary Treasurer, Sir Richard Faber, would not make such claims for the writings of Sir William Temple. Nevertheless, Temple's essays and his elegant style greatly influenced English prose in the 18th century and was much admired by Johnson and Lord Chesterfield. Sir Richard, an ex-diplomat in the Netherlands, shows an obvious affinity with Temple in his admiration for the Dutch. His absorbing lecture was also designed in part to mark an anniversary, the tercentenary of the Glorious Revolution of 1688. These days perhaps Temple is most remembered for the great love between him and Dorothy Osborne, but it was he who brought about the Triple Alliance and the marriage of William of Orange and Mary. His book on the Netherlands moulded opinion in favour of an Anglo-Dutch alliance against the menace of French ambitions for over a quarter of a century.

Dr Gillian Beer is Reader in Literature and Narrative in the University of Cambridge, and I would not presume to synthesize her important lecture given as a joint venture between the Royal Society of Literature, The Royal Society and the British Academy. As she says, our present situation, related to literature and science, differs from that described by C. P. Snow in *The Two Cultures* in 1959. Her

introduction, issued before the lecture, is a helpful preliminary, and I
shall therefore quote it in full:

> Vigorous interchange of ideas and concerns between scientific and
> literary communities should not lead us to expect through-going
> and sustained congruity. Ideas rarely remain intact when they
> change generic context and their reception outside the immediate
> circle of co-workers may raise previously excluded questions.
> Changes of form as well as semantics shape meaning. Scientific
> methods and ideas are often at their most powerful in literary works
> where it is possible to loosen terminology and punningly transgress
> the terms provided. Tensions inhere in the very insistence on single
> signification in scientific discourse. Our analysis may founder if we
> seek a systematic representation of scientific theory within works of
> literature, or indeed a sufficient 'source' of scientific ideas within
> the common structure. The lecture examines, with examples, kinds
> of interchange between scientific and literary texts in the
> nineteenth-century and in our own time.

It was to be expected that Nigel Nicolson's lecture would be a
popular event, and his audience was not disappointed by his brilliant
and amusing references to the editing of his father's diaries and
Virginia Woolf's letters. We all guessed what his attitude would be to
the telephone's 'eternal silence'. Walpole was one of the few who
wrote letters consciously for publication, but 'the best of them, as
Dorothy Osborne was the first to discover, are conversational, cajoling, goading, contradictory, exaggerating, affectionate, funny and
teasing by turns'. Nigel Nicolson puts in a plea that we should
keep up our diaries as a daily discipline, so long as we do not emulate
George V, or that lady who wrote 'I shall never forget that day!' and
now has not the faintest recollection of what actually happened.

And so finally to Maurice Cranston on Voltaire, another evening
much enjoyed, as was the case some years back when he lectured on
Voltaire's adversary Rousseau. If Sir William Temple's residence
in the Netherlands inspired him to write admiringly of the Dutch, so
some sixty years later, Voltaire became an Anglophile after living in
England (with, of course, reservations about our food and weather).
The French had by then patched up some of their differences with the
English, but the French state's policies were resulting in despotism,
persecution, censorship and unjust taxation. One reads Voltaire's

words, quoted by Maurice Cranston, with a certain smugness there-fore:

> In England freedom and prosperity thrive together. Toleration is
> the fruit of liberty, the origin of happiness and abundance. When
> there is not freedom of thought, there is no freedom of trade,
> because the same tyranny encroaches on commerce and religion
> alike. In England, freedom has enlarged commerce, and commerce
> by enriching the people has extended their freedom and the great-
> ness of the state.

A message to be framed and hung in the Cabinet room of 10 Downing
Street, for all future generations, no doubt?

RALEIGH TREVELYAN

Wedmore Memorial Lecture

VOLTAIRE AND THE FREEDOM OF THE PRESS

MAURICE CRANSTON FRSL

Read 8 March 1990
John Guest, FRSL, in the Chair

VOLTAIRE first burst into print at the age of sixteen with a decidedly uncharacteristic work, an *Ode sur Sainte-Geneviève*. I do not know whether that patron saint of Paris can be thought to have interceded on his behalf, for he did go on to acquire great fame and a substantial fortune, and to live to the age of 84. But he gave every appearance always of living on his wits, and if he believed in the omnipotence of God he did not believe in God's benevolence.

Soon after the publication of that first pious ode Voltaire left the school of Louis-le-Grand and started, reluctantly, to study law. He relieved the tedium of those studies by writing more poetry. At first he stuck to respectable subjects, such as *le voeu de Louis XIII* and *les malheurs du temps*; but soon he was producing more dangerous, and more 'voltairian' verses—I say 'voltairian' although he had not yet changed his name from Arouet to Voltaire—an *Épitre à monsieur l'Abbé Servien,* lamenting the fact that imprisonment had separated that worthy priest from his homosexual lover and another *Épitre* to the Bishop of Luçon, commiserating with him on the death of his mistress.

These verses convinced Voltaire's father—an ambitious *bon*

bourgeois, that his son was being corrupted by the smart friends he was making in Paris, so he sent him to live in Caen. But, of course, provincial life is no protection against vice, and in Caen Voltaire fell into the company of some disreputable Jesuits and frequented the salon of Mme d'Osseville, a literary lady who was soon suspected by Voltaire's father of seducing his 19-year-old son.

I am inclined to think the father was wrong about that, because Mme d'Osseville was remarkably ugly, as she herself recognized in an autobiographical poem:

> La maigreur a fait un cruel ravage
> Sur mon corps et sur mon visage

However, Voltaire's father reacted by sending him even further away, to The Hague in Holland, where Voltaire disgraced himself again by trying to elope with the daughter, known as La Pimpette, of an adventuress called Mme Du Noyer. The elopement was thwarted, but after that Voltaire never proposed to another woman for the rest of his life, even though La Pimpette lost no time in marrying another young man.

While he was in Holland, Voltaire noticed something he was to reflect on more fully when he came to England a few years later: the freedom of the press. The Dutch, he observed, were an exceedingly busy and prosperous trading nation. Commerce was not regulated by the government as it was in France, and one element of that free commerce was a free press. Dutch printers and publishers brought out anything they considered profitable, including a great many books which were exported to France, some to be sold openly, more to go to the vast black market. A feature of Dutch publishing that Voltaire also noticed was that an author might actually be paid. In France, that seldom happened.

Even so, when he returned to Paris at the age of twenty, Voltaire declared—to the horror of his father—that he was going to be a full-time poet. He set to work on several grand projects—a tragedy, an epic and a history. He also resumed the writing of light satirical verses, for the accession of the Duc d'Orleans as Regent had introduced a period of licence, not to say debauchery, in which it was safer to publish indecent verse than anything heretical or politically radical. Voltaire took advantage of the situation by producing, among other things, *Épitres* addressed to the Duc d'Arenberg and Prince Eugène congratulating them on their sexual prowess and another to *une Dame très dévote* reproaching her for quitting his bed in a hurry in order to go to confession.

> Dans ta jeunesse fait l'amour
> Et ton salut dans ta vieillesse

Here we can recognize already the voice of Voltaire. But he went too far in a verse addressed to the Duchesse de Berry proclaiming in as many words that she was sleeping with her father. This was unfortunate, in that her father was none other than the Regent himself; and doubly unfortunate in that the accusation was almost certainly true. We cannot be surprised that the poet soon found himself a prisoner in the Bastille; and there, for eleven months, he remained. It was not an uncomfortable place, despite its horrific image in popular mythology. The prisoners were generally superior people—noblemen, writers, booksellers and publishers, for example, and it was not crowded. Prisoners could have their own servants serve their meals and attend to their needs, and cells were spacious. For a writer it was in many ways an ideal situation, especially for one so easily distracted by the pleasures of the salon and the alcove as Voltaire was. In the Bastille Voltaire was able to dedicate himself to serious writing. He found a more decorous way of dealing with the subject of incest than that of Mme de Berry: he wrote a tragedy in verse for the stage about Oedipus.

Six months after his release from the Bastille, his *Oedipe* was performed in Paris, and was a tremendous success. Voltaire, as he had started to call himself, was now at the age of 24 a national celebrity. He became the lion of fashionable society; passing his time, as he put it, moving from château to château. The grand friends he made included Lord Bolingbroke and Lord Stair, who advised him to send an inscribed copy of *Oedipe* to George I. The King responded promptly with a gift of a gold watch and a gold medal; and what a pleasure it is to recall in the Royal Society of Literature how generously the Hanoverian monarchy rewarded poetry; and what a good investment it was, for with that gift King George made Voltaire a passionate Anglophile for life: the greatest propagandist of the century became a propagandist of all things English. Voltaire handed the gold watch to his father as proof that literature was as respectable a trade as law, and watched the old man die a few weeks later, no longer discontented with his son.

In 1722, at the age of 28, Voltaire paid a second visit to Holland, this time to arrange for the publication of his second substantial work, an epic poem titled *La Ligue* about the reign of Henri IV. Unlike *Oedipe*, which was modelled on the tragedies of Racine, and was deliberately cast in a classical mould which was already becoming rather old-fashioned, *La Ligue* belongs to the literature of the Enlightenment. It glorifies Henri IV as the enemy of religious fanaticism and the champion of toleration. It portrays the Catholic and the Protestant faiths as equally sound—or perhaps, equally unsound—and it pleads for freedom. Of course it could not be published in France, but enough copies reached the black market to assure Voltaire of another success. He even attended the marriage of Louis XV, where three of his short plays were performed as part of the celebrations.

He made still more friends in royal and noble households, and being treated there as an equal began to think of himself as an equal. He was to learn, painfully, that he was not one.

The Chevalier de Rohan-Chabot disliked Voltaire intensely, prob-ably because he was jealous of Voltaire's mistress, Mlle Lecouvreur, who was on the stage. At the Opera one evening, the Chevalier kept addressing the writer as 'Monsieur de Voltaire, or Monsieur Arouet, or whatever you call yourself'. Finally, Voltaire replied, sharply: 'I am the first of the Voltaires, just as you are the last of the Rohans.' The remark stung, because the name of Rohan had come to the Chevalier only through his maternal grandmother, and the family name had really been Chabot for two generations. The Chevalier wanted re-venge, but, as he considered Voltaire too low in station to meet in a duel, he had him whipped by his servants. Voltaire was badly beaten up, but the worst part of the experience was his discovery afterwards that none of his noble friends would defend him against Rohan-Chabot. Indeed, when Voltaire spoke of taking revenge, the nobility rallied together and Voltaire was put in the Bastille once again. Fortunately his aristocratic friends from England, Lord Bolingbroke and Lord Stair, proved more loyal, and Voltaire was able to obtain his release from the Bastille on giving an undertaking that he would go into exile. Thus it was in the early summer of 1726 that Voltaire found himself in London. From there he wrote enthusiastically to one of his French friends:

> This is a country where all the arts are honoured and rewarded, a country where are there differences in rank, but only those based on merit, a country where one thinks freely and nobly without being

held back by any servile fear. If I were to follow my inclination, I would settle here, if only for the purpose of learning how to think properly. Here I live among a people fond of their liberty, learned, witty, indifferent to life and death, a nation of philosophers.

England then was a very different place from what it is now. Literary men were not only respected in society, they were given important positions in the state. Prior and Gay had embassies, Addison had the office of Secretary of State: Rowe, Philips and Congreve all had government jobs with very few duties attached to them.

One celebrated poet who had no such place was Alexander Pope and that was because he was a Roman Catholic. Voltaire was too enthusiastic an Anglophile, and too little in love with the Catholic Church, to mind about this. Catholics such as Pope were tolerated in England, he noted, as Protestants were *not* tolerated in France; and he suggested that the French would do well to treat their Protestants as the English treated their Catholics; even though that fell short of full civil liberty.

Soon after he arrived in England Voltaire set about enlarging his poem *La Ligue* into an even larger work now called *La Henriade* and he soon found an English publisher for it, despite the fact that the text was in French.

Voltaire received permission to dedicate the *Henriade* to Queen Caroline, and the book was so successful that it had to be reprinted three times in three weeks. He also brought out special limited editions for book collectors, both French and English; and, making, for once, a decent amount of money out of the book, he became a more enthusiastic Anglophile than ever—as he explained in a letter he wrote in English to a French friend:

> I think and I write like a free Englishman. I heartily wish to see you and my other French friends, but I had rather see them in England than in France. You should cross the Channel to see me. I assure you again that a man of your temper would not dislike a country where one obeys the laws only, and one's own whims.

The list of subscribers to *La Henriade*, printed in the preliminary pages, is a roll call of the English nobility of the time: the Earl of Peterboro, 20 books, the Earl of Chesterfield, 10 books, William Pulteney, 5 books, the Earl of Sussex, 2 books, and so on. George II proved as benevolent as George I, and gave Voltaire a hundred guineas. Voltaire was particularly glad to have the money, because London was such an expensive city to live in:

> When I first arrived in England, I received more invitations than I could possibly afford to accept. The trouble was that whenever one went to dine at a house in London, the servants would line up in the hall, waiting to be tipped, and the tips would amount to more than the price of a meal in a tavern.

The food was one of the things Voltaire began to tire of in London. He was accustomed to dining in France at the tables of his grand friends, who kept the best cooks in the world. English cooking, which had once been much better than the French, already began to decline in the eighteenth century. In matters of food, Voltaire was not easy to please. He also came to dislike the English climate, which he considered too damp. Moreover, there was a certain puritanism about the English which Voltaire simply could not understand:

> Considering how prosperous England is, the standard of living is very low. London is the rival of Paris in size, but by no means its rival in splendour, or taste or amusement or the arts of society. I believe that there is five hundred times more silver plate in the private houses of Paris than in those of London. In Paris a mere notary or attorney or wool merchant is better housed, has much better furniture, and is much better served than a great magistrate in London. The English are rich, but they do not enjoy their riches.

Perhaps it is not altogether surprising that, as soon as it was safe for Voltaire to return to Paris, he went home. Even so, he took back with him from his two years in London two lasting enthusiasms—one for English literature, the other for English political ideas. He could never quite bring himself to approve of Shakespeare. But for the most part he thought that English literature was magnificent, and late in his life he claimed that he had been its most effective champion in France:

> It was I who introduced English literature to France. Before I translated parts of Milton, Dryden and Alexander Pope, no one in France knew anything of English poetry. As for English philosophy, I was the first to explain Newton and Locke. And Jonathan Swift, the Rabelais of English literature—he would never have been read in France but for my efforts.

Voltaire is here perhaps making an exaggerated boast. Madame Du Châtelet did more than he to introduce, by her translations, the work of Newton to the French public. But, as Voltaire was her lover, taught her English, and lived with her for several years, he could be excused for thinking that what Madame Du Châtelet knew about Newton she had learned from him. As for the philosopher Locke, what Voltaire took from him was chiefly the belief that men have natural rights to life, liberty and property. But the English philosopher who had really had the greatest influence on Voltaire was neither Locke nor Newton, but the Lord Chancellor Francis Bacon, a contemporary in the early seventeenth century of Voltaire's royal hero, Henri IV.

What excited Voltaire in Bacon was Bacon's doctrine that science might save mankind. The great merit of science, in Bacon's eyes, was that it could be applied, in practical ways, to solve all men's problems on earth. Scientific research could be used to improve agriculture, and so provide men with enough to eat. Science could be applied to medicine, and so help overcome the diseases which did so much to diminish men's joy on earth. Science could be used to solve all the technical problems of housing, transport, industrial production, and so forth, which, being unsolved, had hitherto kept men in a miserable condition. Bacon further argued that the reign of science required two conditions. First, that all old-fashioned philosophical and religious thinking should be discarded. Secondly, it required strong, systematic central government.

These ideas Voltaire took over, more or less entirely, from Bacon —the political as well as the ideological part. It would be unfair to say that Voltaire learned from Bacon the gospel of 'enlightened despotism', although that is something which is often attributed to Voltaire. But he certainly accepted the doctrine of absolute government: the idea of a strong regime, directed to the public good by a scientifically minded, or philosophically minded, king.

In his history of *L'Ancien régime* Tocqueville makes what I think a very fair criticism of Voltaire on this point. He says that Voltaire praises the liberty of the press in England without recognising that that liberty depended on the English system of parliamentary government, which Voltaire did not like at all, Voltaire thinking that Parliament was dominated by the aristocratic interest that he detested so much. Voltaire was content to ascribe the merits of English Government to the virtues of English Kings.

The most noted exponent of the idea that the French government should be remodelled on the lines of the English parliamentary system was the Baron de Montesquieu, whose marvellous *Persian Letters* can claim precedence over Voltaire's *Henriade* as the first book of the Enlightenment. Montesquieu was five years older than Voltaire, and he made his name as a writer at much the same time as Voltaire made his. Voltaire's attitude to Montesquieu was always that of a rival —and, although he agreed with Montesquieu in many ways, and certainly shared his love of all things English, Voltaire mistrusted Montesquieu, and he took no pleasure in agreeing with him. He suspected that Montesquieu wished to reform the French constitution on the English model only to serve his class interests. Montesquieu, a member both of the *noblesse de robe* and the *noblesse de race* favoured the English form of the Houses of Parliament, Voltaire suspected, only because the House of Lords gave considerable advantages to peers. Voltaire, for his part, was keenly conscious of the interests of his own class, the bourgeoisie. The thrashings he had received from the servants of the Chevalier de Rohan-Chabot had left Voltaire with an unyielding hatred of hereditary privilege. His policy in life was to dine with the dukes and think with the merchants.

As soon as he got back to France he started to write a series of letters on the English, afterwards known as *Les Lettres philosophiques*. This promptly put him at odds with the system of literary censorship in France. This vast, complicated, elaborate and rather absurd structure had been set up by the Bourbon monarchy in the seventeenth century. At the head of it was a magistrate of the Versailles government called the Director of Publications. One of these Directors, Malesherbes explained in a moment of frankness how it worked. The Director had a team of censors reading material whose number rose from 40 to 178 in Voltaire's lifetime and on their advice the Director could in the first place licence a book that was really safe with a *privilège*. Alternatively he could give tacit permission either for publication or for the importing of a more dubious book. But such permission was not really tacit as it had to be registered. Or again, the Director might promise to close his eyes to the existence of a book, a sort of tacit, tacit permission. And of course there were clandestine publications of which he was genuinely unaware.

Certain Directors of Publication, including Malesherbes, were in full sympathy with writers such as Montesquieu and Voltaire: and indeed Voltaire received tacit permission for the sale of *La Ligue* and *La Henriade*. However, there were other agencies of censorship in

France besides the office of Publications: these were the *parlements*, who sometimes acted against books and authors who had something less than a full *privilege* from the Director of Publications, and the clerical authorities at the Sorbonne did the same: the parlement persecuted Rousseau for *Emile* and the Sorbonne persecuted Helvétius for *De l'esprit*.

Voltaire showed the manuscript of his *Lettres philosophiques* to one of the censors, and was told he would never be allowed to publish the book. Nevertheless he had it printed secretly, and by April 1734 copies were on the black market. In May, the government issued a *lettre de cachet* for Voltaire's arrest, apprehended and imprisoned the printer, and on the orders of the Paris *parlement* the public executioner lacerated and burned the book in the courtyard of the *Palais de Justice*. But they did not catch Voltaire. He had departed from Paris to find refuge on the borders of Lorraine, and henceforth he kept clear of Paris for most of the rest of his life. In rustic exile, he became an even more prolific author than he had been in the Bastille. It has been calculated that he wrote between fourteen and sixteen million words for publication. Besides this remarkable industry, Voltaire possessed enormous cunning, and he used it both to protect himself, and to exploit the chaos and incompetence which prevailed in the censorship to get his books published, in the interstices of an irrational system, playing Jesuits against Jansenists, Versailles against the *parlements*, the state against the church. But he never again stuck his neck out, as Diderot did, much to Voltaire's alarm, by publishing the Encyclopaedia in Paris instead of in Holland.

Events in eighteenth century Europe encouraged Voltaire to develop the idea of enlightened absolutism; for there appeared on the thrones of Europe in his lifetime several princes who yearned to be at the same time absolute and enlightened: notably the Austrian Emperor, the Empress of Russia, the King of Poland and the King of Prussia, and all of them fervent readers of Voltaire's published works. One of them, Frederick of Prussia, went so far as to write to Voltaire, imploring him to come to Potsdam and be his guide.

Voltaire accepted an invitation and went to live for a time at his court in Potsdam. But the visit was not a success. He found that Frederick had no desire to receive the advice of a philosopher or govern his kingdom on lines suggested to him by Voltaire. He wanted Voltaire to help him in his literary endeavours, to criticise—or rather, to praise—his poems. What was worse, Frederick embarked on policies which Voltaire most detested, building up a powerful army and then going to war.

Voltaire was often simply baffled by the moral sentiments of his contemporaries. They were shocked by things that did not shock him: and in turn he was shocked by things that did not shock them. He was amazed, for example, at the fuss people made about cannibalism, in view of their indifference to killing on the scaffold or the battlefield.

We kill our neighbours in pitched or unpitched battles, and so prepare meals for the crows and the worms. That is the horror. That is the crime. It is not in putting a man on the spit when he is dead that is evil: it is killing a man in the first place.

War was accepted by many people almost as a law of nature, one of the regularities of human experience, like the rising and setting of the sun, or the succession of the seasons. Voltaire tried to make people understand that there was no necessity about war, or many other evils which men chose to inflict upon their fellows. People had even a habit, Voltaire suggested, of inventing crimes to increase their misery on earth—the crime of sorcery, for example:

What is this crime of sorcery? It is a fantasy created by religious imaginations. If there is no law against sorcery, there is no crime of sorcery. And when such laws have been abolished—as they have been abolished in Prussia, England, Holland and Venice—there is no more witchcraft. It is a disgrace to our own Kingdom that sorcery remains a crime in France.

After years of wandering Voltaire found happiness in a home of his own, a chateau he bought at Ferney on the borders of Geneva. At Ferney he offered lavish hospitality to various friends and refugees, and started factories to provide employment for local workers. He came to like his Swiss neighbours, and even expressed admiration for the kind of democracy which prevailed in the rural parts of that country:

I like to see free men make the laws under which they live, just as they make the houses in which they live. It pleases me that my mason, my carpenter, my blacksmith, my neighbour the farmer and my friend the manufacturer all raise themselves above their trade, and they know the public interest better than the most insolent Turkish satrap. In a democracy, no labourer, no artisan, need fear either molestation or contempt. To be free and equal is the natural life of man.

Voltaire admired the democratic Swiss, but he was too sophisticated a man—and too completely French—to have enjoyed living permanently in a democratic Swiss society. He occupied for a time a small villa in Geneva itself, which, preserved today as a museum and institute to commemorate his work is a place well worth a visit. But the city of Calvin was certainly not the natural home for a man of Voltaire's temperament. He even caused a storm by suggesting that there ought to be an opera house in Geneva to brighten up the life of the place. The suggestion was ill received. In any case, Voltaire built his own little theatre where his own plays could be acted at Ferney. Ferney had the great advantage of being on French soil but being within a few minutes' distance of the Swiss frontier, should Voltaire ever need to escape from the hand of the French law. But no one could accuse Voltaire of lacking in French patriotism. Indeed his love of France was so intense that, when he looked back as a historian to the seventeenth century, he was disposed to forgive the faults of the Bourbon kings because of their achievements.

Louis XIV did not do all he might have done—no doubt because he was a man—but he did more than any other, because he was a great man. It is true that he drove the Protestants from France, but they found refuge in England, and enriched that nation with the wealth of French industry. Give me the name of any sovereign who attracted more foreigners to his country, and did more to encourage merit among his own subjects. Under Louis XIV, all the arts were perfected, and all were rewarded. Not only were great things done during his reign; it was he who did them.

Voltaire wrote three very substantial works of history: *The Century of Louis XIV*, about his own country; the *History of Charles XII*, about Sweden; and a *History of the Russian Empire*. They are all written in his marvellous clear style, salted by his unmistakable wit, but as works of history they are decidedly romantic, centring on the personalities of the kings and emperors who play the central role in the events described.

There is an obvious contradiction between this romantic, even sentimental, royalist side of Voltaire, and the liberal side; but the interesting thing is that Voltaire didn't make any attempt to resolve the contradiction. He seems in fact to have been scarcely aware of it. In a sense, he was much too absorbed in protesting against what was wrong with existing arrangements to give a systematic form to his philosophy. This must be reckoned a defect; it may also be one of the secrets of Voltaire's success. He does not brood on the nature of justice. He simply feels what injustice is, and that is enough. Injustice cries out. And it does not cry out to be understood, but rather to be noticed, and remedied. But he never lost his self-control. He attacked the enemy, not with passion, but with irony. Lord Chesterfield once wrote to congratulate him on his restraint.

> Above all, Monsieur, I am grateful to you for the light in which you place the lunacy and frenzy of the sects. You employ the proper weapons against these madmen and impostors; to employ others against them would be to imitate them: it is with ridicule that they must be attacked; it is with contempt that they must be punished.

Voltaire was delighted to find in the economic theorists of his time confirmation of his own belief that private luxury coincides with the public interests. One of his favourite economists was J. F. Mélon, who argues in his *Essai sur le commerce* that commerce consists in the exchange of what is superfluous for what is necessary. The more prosperous a nation, the more advantage it will gain from trading with other nations. Commerce elevates a country from savage customs to the benefits of civilisation. The wealth acquired by one section of a society will have repercussions for all the other sections. The high consumption of *some* will provide a profitable market for the production of others. The desire of each to increase his well-being will lead to the enjoyment of luxury, which Mélon defines as 'extraordinary sumptuosity produced by wealth and secure government'. With the passage of time yesterday's luxuries become today's necessities: and thus the innocent pursuit and enjoyment of luxury becomes a motive of general progress.

Voltaire not only read Mélon, he also read Bernard Mandeville, and was at the same time attracted and repelled. If Voltaire's poem in defence of luxury *La Mondain* reproduces the arguments of Mélon, its sequel, *La Defense du mondain* is closer to Mandeville, but Mandeville without his naked cynicism.

Mandeville, as Voltaire understood him, maintained that it is vice that keeps the economic system moving. The vanity of women made them demand more and more clothing, more elaborate and original styles of clothing every season; and this is what keeps the textile industry active together with the wholesalers and retailers of clothes. The greed of men makes them demand even greater refinement in their food and drink, and this generates business for farmers and vintners and purveyors of every sort. The avarice of merchants prompts them to risk their capital in the hope of gain, and this makes industry and commerce possible. Even the dishonesty of thieves makes work for locksmiths and policemen.

Voltaire with his special reverence for property was particularly scandalised by this last suggestion. After all, he protested, there was poison in many medicines but that did not mean that poison could be praised as what cured patients. However, under the influence of Madame Du Chatelet, who admired Mandeville to the point of translating his work into French, Voltaire came to see more merit in *The Fable of the Bees.*

Mandeveille's argument was that men cannot have both the comforts of life and virtue and innocence. The comforts of life—luxury, wealth, power—were the products of vice. A virtuous people according to Mandeville would not do much or change much; a virtuous people would be frugal, public-spirited, and weak; they would have no dynamic, nothing would motivate their economy. On the other hand, a vicious people, greedy for more and more private satisfaction would be active, industrious, adventurous, and their economy would therefore become prosperous and powerful.

It pleased Voltaire that Mandeville should cut short the cackle and the cant about virtue; but Voltaire, for all his scepticism, was not a cynic. He took an altogether more kindly view of man's sociability than did Mandeville. He believed that men acquired altruistic habits as a result of living in families, and that nature had instilled in everyone both compassion for others and a *bienveillance générale.* He could not accept Mandeville's suggestion that morality was bred entirely from the so-called vice of pride, society exacting good behaviour from its members only by making them ashamed of being ill-regarded by their neighbours. Indeed, Voltaire refused to treat as vices what Mandeville considered vices, or as virtues what Mandeville called virtues. While he agreed with Mandeville that Athens, the city of luxury was in every way preferable to Sparta, the city of austerity, he could see no evidence of greater virtue among the Spartans; on the contrary, he regarded Sparta, with its militarism and regimentation and its massacres, as morally repugnant. In the end he came to see Mandeville—a Dutchman who wrote in English—as an inverted Calvinist, taking Calvin's conception of what virtue is and then mocking virtue. Voltaire had an altogether different conception of virtue: right or good actions were those which either diminished the amount of suffering in the world or which increased the amount of happiness. He insisted on the importance of keeping the province of the law separate from that of morality. Prisons and penalties should not be used as forms of retribution, but as a means of deterrence and reform. Society must protect itself, but no man should assume the office of God and inflict punishment on sinners. Penalties could be justified only in terms of utility. The death penalty was rarely, if ever justified: and torture was as useless as it was odious.

'No opinions, beliefs, or thoughts can be criminal: only acts can be crimes'. Consequently, Voltaire argued, 'all punishments for religious, philosophical or even political opinions are unfair.'

He once described himself as an 'Epicurean'. 'Stoicism' he wrote, 'is undoubtedly better than Christian moral teaching. It breeds a better character. A Stoic must earn salvation by living well, whereas a Christian needs only a last-minute repentance after thirty years of crime to be assured of eternal bliss. But I am not a Stoic. I am rather an Epicurean. I do not think life is to be endured: I think it is to be enjoyed'.

In his later years Voltaire moved closer to Stoicism, but it would perhaps be better to describe him with a modern word as a utilitarian. He did not seek happiness for himself alone; he wanted it for everyone. The famous formula of Cesare Beccaria, *la massima felicitá del massimo numero*, was one which well expressed Voltaire's own measure of the good, and Jeremy Bentham, who corresponded with Voltaire, acknowledged him as his 'master'. Even so, Voltaire did not carry his utilitarianism to the lengths of those theorists who believed that the elimination of poverty should be a matter of public policy and that the state should tax the rich in order to redistribute wealth among the poor. One of the reasons why he admired Locke so much was that Locke took such care to justify a natural right to property, and put that right together with the rights to life and liberty. When Voltaire read Rousseau's *Discourse on the Origin of Inequality* one of the things which enraged him most was Rousseau's suggestion that the right to property was somehow fraudulent: 'What!' Voltaire wrote in the margin of his text, 'has a man no right to the fruit of his labour?'

Voltaire was very much a man of property. In the course of a long life, he made a great deal of money; some of it by shrewd organisation of the publication of his book, some by inheritance from his father, much more by shrewd investment, by lending money at usurious rates of interest to hard-up noblemen, and some by luck in a lottery—if 'luck' is the word for finding a loophole in the rules which enabled him to sweep in the winnings.

Towards the end of his life he said that he had once thought nothing of money, but had then seen so many men of letters poor and despised that he resolved not to augment their number: 'I turned myself into a hammer to avoid being used as an anvil. The first efforts to make money are painful, but it soon becomes very satisfying to watch one's property accumulate, and in old age, where money is most necessary, it is almost a duty to be rich'.

Voltaire was an optimist. *Candide*, the full title of which is *Candide, ou l'Optimisme*, makes spirited fun of a certain kind of optimist, the view put forward by Alexander Pope in his *Essay on Man* that this world is the best of possible worlds; but optimism in another, and perhaps more ordinary, sense Voltaire consistently upholds. That is to say, Voltaire believes the world is getting better and better. In his *Essay on Morals*, he claims that human history is a continuous movement of human progress through the gradual enlargement of human knowledge. In other words, Voltaire is saying that, what Bacon wanted to happen, will happen.

The only uncertainty about Voltaire's kind of optimism is the kind of action it calls for. At the end of *Candide*, he recommends a form of quietism. We must each cultivate our garden. It is no good bothering one's head with useless metaphysical questions: one must make life acceptable by absorbing oneself in one's own work. But other writings of Voltaire recommend something much more active. And indeed the whole life of the polemicist that he himself lived is a denial of the idea that we ought each to cultivate our own garden.

But Voltaire did not take his own advice. At the age of seventy he became an almost full-time campaigner for toleration, and published, among other things, the celebrated *Traité sur la tolérance*. What prompted him to publish this work was a revival of religious fanaticism in France, which was not entirely unlike the fanaticism we observe in Islam today. When a Protestant pastor, and a group of his friends were executed in Toulouse for holding a religious assembly, and Protestant laymen in the same part of France were victimized on trumped-up criminal charges, Voltaire came to feel that the kind of iconoclastic and anticlerical writings on behalf of freedom that he had been pouring out in such abundance were having little effect on readers who didn't already share his scepticism, and that it was necessary to make the case for toleration in terms which would appeal to believe and unbelievers alike. When the wave of persecution in Toulouse first began, Voltaire reacted with his usual flippant cynicism. Told that Pastor Rochette had been hanged for holding a Calvinist service with the chanting of psalms, he remarked brightly that it was a very harsh sentence for singing bad verses. But he did at least write to the Duc de Richelieu to plead for clemency, which is more than Rousseau did when he was asked to intervene on behalf of the same unfortunate pastor.

What really spurred Voltaire to action was the next case against a Protestant in Toulouse: the execution of Jean Calas on the extraordinary charge of murdering his own son in order to prevent him converting to Catholicism. This time Voltaire did not hear about the case until after Calas has been put to death, but once he took it up, he would not let it rest. He paid investigators to root out the evidence and lawyers to study the trial. He was soon convinced that there had been a gross miscarriage of justice. Calas had been at home with every other member of his family, a servant and a visitor at the time when his son died by hanging. The son had probably committed suicide; if he was murdered, no member of the Calas family could have murdered him unless they had all participated, together with the servant and the visitor. No impartial court could have found Jean Calas along guilty as charged. The court at Toulouse, Voltaire decided, was *not* impartial; it was prejudiced against Calas because he was a Protestant, not just prejudiced but blinded by the anti-Protestant fanaticism which seemed to be sweeping the whole region of Toulouse. Several orders of monks, Voltaire discovered, had been holding public ceremonies and processions in the streets with hooded robes and sacred relics designed to stimulate fear and hatred of Protestants, and the frenzy spread alike among the clergy and laity, among the uneducated and the educated, until it reached the magistrates themselves.

Voltaire was tireless in his efforts to prove that Calas had been a victim of injustice; he wrote innumberable letters to influential person at Versailles and after a campaign of several years he succeeded in getting the verdict reversed and Calas's name cleared by a royal court of appeal. But Calas was not the last victim. A new case developed in the same part of France, when yet another Protestant, one Pierre Sirven, was accused of murdering his daughter from the same motive as that of Calas. She had been undergoing Catholic instruction in a convent, and she was found dead in a well. Unlike Calas, Sirven escaped with his family to Switzerland, where he threw himself at the feet of Voltaire. This time Voltaire did not simply intervene with the authorities on behalf of the accused. He decided to address his French compatriots in general by publishing a plea for toleration, speaking as a Catholic to Catholics with arguments which as Christians ought to understand. At the same time his appeal rested on principles which any reasonable person, whether Christian or not, should appreciate.

The basis of Voltaire's argument in his *Traité sur la tolérance* is that man is too *insignificant* a creature to be able to know the mind of God, too *limited* in his faculties even to understand fully the things of his own experience. Our world, as Voltaire puts it, is but a tiny point in space, and man is lost in all this immensity. We are miniscule units in the universe; each of us a little ant among the nine hundred million other little ants that constitute the human race. So what are we to say to the little ant who asserts: 'My ant-hill is dear to God, and the other ant-hills are not; some are even reprobated by Him'?

And yet that claim, Voltaire suggests, is exactly what many human beings make. He tells the story of Frederick of Prussia arriving in a Protestant village in Silesia in the course of one of his wars; the villagers beg him to kill all the inhabitants of a neighbouring village, who are Catholics. The king replies: 'What would you have to say to them if they beg me to kill all of you?' The villagers protest: 'But Sire, *our* religion is the *true* one.'

Well, says Voltaire, every sect may think it has the true religion; but none of them can prove it, so it is best to put up with other sects, however mistaken one believes them to be. Voltaire declared his own assent to the proposition: 'Outside the church there is no salvation'. He respects it, he says, and repeats it, but he denies that it entitles him to say that everyone who is not a Catholic is damned to eternal perdition. In fact, he claims that no sensible Frenchman actually believes such a thing, otherwise there would be no daily commerce between the French and their Protestant neighbours in Switzerland and Germany and England, no public mourning for the death of Protestant sovereigns, and no diplomatic representatives at their Courts, unless the French Ambassador were to say: 'Your Majesty will infallibly burn in hell.'

Voltaire being Voltaire, he can't stop himself from using irony even when he is posing as an obedient Catholic. He describes what he calls the 'merciful mission' of an order of monks in Denmark, who reflect on the Doctrine that an infant is assured of eternal glory if it dies immediately after baptism and before it has been corrupted by original sin. These Danish monks therefore proceed to kill as many newly-baptised children as they can so as to ensure their unhindered entry to paradise. Unfortunately, Voltaire, suggests, these charitable workers make the same mistake as their brethren of the Holy Inquisition who torture and burn heretics for the salvation of their souls. They overlook the principle of natural law which forbids us to do evil for the sake of greater good. The only natural law which authorises killing is the natural law of the tiger: and that allows the tiger only to kill for its own survival; and not for the greater good of the victim.

Much as Erasmus had done in an earlier century, Voltaire argued that the Bible afforded no authority for the persecution of dissenters. Although terrible punishments were authorised in the Old Testament, they were for disobedience, he argued, not for disagreement in belief. The New Testament taught men to love their enemies, not to torture their neighbours. Voltaire also followed Locke in pointing out that force could not succeed in altering a man's secret thoughts, even though it might well produce hypocrites, who would make their outward gestures of conformity, without inward assent. But Voltaire carried the argument a step further than Erasmus and Locke by depicting toleration as a moral *duty* that was imposed on men by their very nature, their vulnerability and their ignorance.

Born without knowledge, a man could only learn truth by a process of inquiry and discussion, listening to the opinions of others and exchanging his thoughts with theirs learning from his mistakes as well as from as discoveries. If a man refuses to listen to what he doesn't want to hear, he runs the risk of not hearing the truth, of denying himself the benefit of criticism and correction, of being left with a head full of stale and very possibly erroneous notions.

Voltaire was careful to remind the world that the Catholics were not the only persecutors. The city of Geneva where he found refuge from the French authorities had its own bloody history. Calvin had put the unitarian Servetus to death for heresy. In Voltaire's time private morality was still being enforced by the Genevese police. One spirited citizen appealed to him when he was instructed to genuflect before the council in the course of a trial for fornication; he protested that genuflection was a degrading practice. Voltaire wrote him a letter addressed to 'Monsieur le Fornicateur' congratulating him on his fortitude.

A more serious case was that of Jean-Jacques Rousseau, threatened with prison and perhaps death for writing *The Social Contract*. Voltaire abominated Rousseau as a person and as a thinker. But in defending him, he demonstrated what toleration is all about— upholding the rights of people you don't like or don't approve of, people who are bound to be ungrateful, because toleration is always a second-best thing to freedom.

But while Voltaire protested at the measures taken in Geneva against Rousseau, he also suggested[1] that Rousseau ought to come back to Geneva and compromise with the authorities. 'Jean-Jacques should return and the syndics will say to him "you have done wrong to write what you have written: promise to respect the religion of your country in future". Jean-Jacques should make that promise and perhaps say that his publisher added certain pages to the book.' The friend of Rousseau, through whom Voltaire transmitted that advice, assured Voltaire that Rousseau would never never disown what he had written.

I suspect that if Voltaire were alive today he might give much the same advice to Salman Rushdie, while at the same time being a good deal less polite than we seem to be towards the Moslem clergy who want to kill him. 'Ecrasez l'infame' today would be 'Ecrasez l'Islam'.

Voltaire had at first the feeling that his *Traité sur la tolérance* was a total failure. Less than three years after its publication there occurred the case which distressed him more than any other and that was the torture and execution of the young Chevalier de la Barre for the crime of singing impious songs on a bridge at Abbeville and passing a procession of Capucins without taking off his hat. The magistrates of Abbeville ordered not only that the young man's tongue be torn out, his hand cut off, and his body burned in a slow fire, but they also put him on the rack to discover how many impious songs he had sung. The *parlement* of Paris reduced the sentence to execution by decapitation, largely out of respect for the chevalier's rank; but his body was ceremoniously burned and a copy of Voltaire's *Philosophical Dictionary* was thrown on the flames to burn with the corpse.

[1] Rousseau, *Correspondance complète* (Ed. Leigh) XI pp. 231–232.

Afterwards Voltaire prepared a new version of the *Philosophical Dictionary* in order to insert the story of the Chevalier de la Barre, and to summarise once more the case for toleration that he had expounded in his Treatise. This time he was able to point out to his French readers that the Empress Catherine of Russia had just introduced laws that abolished torture and established universal toleration, which, as he put it, left the French behind in the darkness, the most barbarian nation in Europe. At last Voltaire began to feel that people were listening to what he had to say. Public opinion changed in France after the death of the Chevalier de la Barre and Voltaire had probably done more than any single individual to change it. When he returned to Paris just before his death in 1778 he was hailed by the crowd, less as a writer than as a champion of freedom and toleration and the rights of man, the defender of the persecuted; the hero of the liberal hour.

Back in the year 1694, when Voltaire was born, the French had no reason to disbelieve that their Kingdom was the greatest in the world—in the military, intellectual, artistic, scientific fields. France was ahead, even of England, which had spent so much of its energy in the seventeenth century in civil war and social conflicts. But in the eighteenth century the English had patched up their quarrels and gone far ahead of the French in industrial, scientific, economic and political achievements; as Voltaire observed:

> In England freedom and prosperity thrive together. Toleration is the fruit of liberty, the origin of happiness and of abundance. When there is no freedom of thought, there is no freedom of trade, because the same tyranny encroaches on commerce and religion alike. In England, freedom has enlarged commerce, and commerce, by enriching the people, has extended their freedom and furthered the greatness of the state.

England, as an island of freedom and prosperity, was a standing reproach to a France which was doing badly in war, and worse in peace, which was backward, and on the verge of bankruptcy. The French state preached the ideas of glory and honour, but provided only humiliation, despotism, religious persecution, censorship and a manifestly unjust system of taxation. Against such a background, the gospel of Voltaire found a naturally responsive public: the English, who read him as eagerly as the French, were reassured that they were on the right lines: the French were excited by the prospect of something better than what they had to endure.

Many ideas of the Enlightenment have rightly fallen into disrepute: the gospel of progress, the faith in science, the triumph of reason—all these are seen today to be shop-soiled slogans. But one achievement of Voltaire no one can deny: he awakened in his readers a very real feeling—and a very valuable feeling—of compassion for their fellow men; instilled in others his own hatred of persecution and fanaticism and cruelty. Voltaire never thought of himself as recommending anything at all utopian. He only wanted his contemporaries to combine the advantages of French culture with the benefits of English experience, to give up persecution and war, and learn to be at once prosperous and free.

There is a certain irony in the success of Voltaire's *Traité sur la tolérance*. He helped to put an end to religious intolerance when religious intolerance was already diminishing together with religious fervour in general. But Voltaire's work did nothing to correct another form of intolerance—ideological intolerance which prompted all the summary executions and massacres of the French Revolution.

But at least the French Revolution abolished all the institutions of Censorship which were part of the *ancien régime*—the Office of Publications, the *parlements*, the clerical census of the Sorbonne. Henceforth the press in France was, except for a few intervals of despotism, about as free as the press in England. That is to say, rather less than completely free, but a good deal more free than it was in Voltaire's lifetime.

Giff Edmonds Memorial Lecture

THE LETTER, THE DIARY AND THE TELEPHONE

NIGEL NICOLSON MBE, FRSL

Read 23 June 1988
Rt Hon Lord Jenkins of Hillhead, FRSL, in the Chair

IN THIS lecture I shall pick here and there at the vast quarry of English letters and diaries, examine the changing motives of their writers, assess how far we should trust them as material for history and biography, and consider whether in the most articulate and self-conscious age the world has ever known, the telephone by its universal use and terminal silence will rob future generations of a knowledge of our times as intimate as that which we derive from the letters and diaries of the past.

Nothing can emulate the record of a scene written down immediately afterwards. In no other way can private conversations be preserved, nor details like the food and drink consumed, by whom, in what quantity, the interruptions, arrivals, departures, the amity or tension of a private party or a formal meeting. And nowhere is a self-portrait more accurately if inadvertently drawn than by a man's daily journal and correspondence, and a woman's too, since for many centuries these were the only literary exercises permitted to them without upsetting men. Psychoanalysts may dispute it, but I defend the proposition that nobody can know us as well as we know ourselves, and how can it be otherwise when every one of us in this room is the only person who will ever know everything we have done and thought since we awoke this morning, and every morning throughout a lifetime? That is the record which a full diary leaves, the black-box that registers every manoeuvre we make till we crash and die.

I am not speaking, of course, of the trivial diary, the sort of diary that even kings can keep, like George V who was content to write, 'Another miserable wet day, even wetter than yesterday. It is earnestly hoped that it will be less wet tomorrow'; nor of such entries as that in the diary of a lady I know, 'I shall never forget this day!': on re-reading it twenty years later she hadn't the faintest recollection of what happened. Such diaries are but daily snapshots or annotated engagement books. No, I am thinking of diaries that provide the author, as Charles Greville wrote of his, with 'constant and brisk amusement', or of Francis Kilvert's, who gave perhaps the best definition of a diary's purpose:

> Life appears to me such a curious and wonderful thing that it almost seems a pity that even such a humble and uneventful life as mine should pass altogether away without some record; and I think the record may amuse and interest some who come after me.

A diary of this kind was an innovation of the seventeenth century. Previous diaries were extraordinarily dull, 'I went into the Courts and had conference with my Lord of Leicester upon a matter of great importance.' That's all we get from Sir Francis Walsingham on a typical day in 1580. And even if we had Shakespeare's diary, it would probably add no more than two percent to our knowledge of him, since the modern formula was beyond even his invention.

The formula is a frank and detailed account of the diarist's daily activities, supplemented by observations on his own conduct and that of other people. A diary is a wineglass to hold his delights, a sump for his despair. Everyone is alternately the hero and the villain of his diary. It leads inevitably to introspection, usually derogatory. Over and over again in our literary history diarists have sought absolution for what they have done or failed to do, castigated themselves for the sins that beset all mankind, and the most frequently mentioned is sloth, of which diary-keeping itself is one manifestation, and the second is how far achievement falls short of aspiration. Boswell felt such contempt for his behaviour that he couldn't even bear to write his diary in the first person, 'How vain and impossible you are!', he would record, and then, giving himself orders, 'So, from hence, never dispute. Be firm. Swear, no woman for a week. Labour hard.' But every resolution is no sooner made than broken, 'At night, a new girl', he writes next day. Then William Windham, a politician of no mean attainment at the turn of the eighteenth century: 'I was tempted to speak on an incidental point in the debate, and succeeded so ill where I think I might have succeeded so well.' Or, on a lower level, Thomas Marchant, a fish-trader of Sussex whose diary Arthur Ponsonby disinterred, wrote on January 19 1728, 'Did nothing but eat and drink and sit by the fire all day, and hard work I found it.' Or Greville, 'When I see what other men have done, how they had read and thought, a sort of despair comes over me.' Or Elizabeth Fry, 'I am a bubble without reason, without beauty of mind or person, I am a fool, I daily fall lower in my own estimation.' The trail of self-pity that runs through even the brightest minds is unending, and the diary, which is the confidant that no wife or husband ever could be, which never betrays, never answers back, never scolds, is its recipient.

Nobody can sustain for long these moods of self-mortification and jealousy, desiring this man's art and that man's scope, and every diarist, except perhaps John Wesley who swore to himself, 'never to laugh, no, not for a moment', rises to moments of exhilaration or self-satisfaction, like Macaulay on his 49th birthday:

> I have no cause for complaint. Tolerable health; competence; liberty; leisure; very dear relations and friends; a great, (I may say, a very great), literary reputation.

Somebody must have been listening for him to put in that 'I may say'. Or Benjamin Robert Haydon, who so despaired of his debts and his failure as an artist that he slit his throat an hour after penning the last words of his brilliant journal, but could write of an expedition to Brighton that he 'rolled in the sea, shouted like a savage, laved my sides like a bull in a green meadow, dived, swam, floated, and came out refreshed.'

Now there speaks the true diarist. The lazy diarist would merely write, 'Went to Brighton, bathed'. For even if a diary is not a work of literature, being unpremeditated and uncorrected, it must give the reader the satisfaction that the writer has revelled in the manifold opportunities of our language, that he is capable of a certain careless rapture, throwing syntax to the winds, like a man knocking up in a squash-court, trying out new shots, bashing the ball about, indifferent to error because he is free from scrutiny. He finds his memory and power of observation sharpened by their exercise, and he lives his daily experiences with subliminal anticipation of how he will describe them that night. When the typewriter arrives, his fingers keep pace with his racing ideas more easily than the pen. His thought-bubbles burst with tiny explosions on the page, most of them wasted or contradicted, because wastage in a diary is something that author and reader come to take for granted.

What is his purpose? Does he write his diary with any other audience in mind than himself in old age? It is possible, I suppose, to imagine a timid lover writing a series of letters he never intends to post, pouring into them the adoration and hopes he never dares express openly for fear that they will not be reciprocated. But he is addressing someone very definite indeed, like a child's letter puffed hopefully up the chimney to Father Christmas. The diarist has no specific correspondent, but it is almost inconceivable that he is talking solely to himself, since all writing is a form of communication, and one cannot communicate with a blank page.

I can best illustrate the diary's mixed motives by my father's, which he kept every day for thirty-four years. From time to time he would ask himself why he was keeping it, and he gave different answers. Eight years after beginning it in 1930, he wrote, 'It is not a work of self-revelation but a mere record of activity put down for my own reference only'. Two years later, in the middle of the London blitz, when his sense of living precariously was most acute, he wrote: 'If I survive, this diary will be for me a record from which I can fill in remembered details, and I find some relief in putting down on paper the momentary spurts and gushes of this cataract of history'. His diary was becoming something subtly different—notes for the autobiography he never wrote, a strainer to catch some of the emotions of the day before they were irretrievably lost. As the war progressed, an actual audience took shape in his mind. 'One should write one's diary', he came to consider, 'for one's great-grandson. The purely private diary becomes too self-centred and morbid. One should have a remote, but not too remote, an audience.' As it turned out, he wrote it for me.

To sustain a diary like Haydon's for sixty years, or Wesley's for sixty-six, or Queen Victoria's for sixty-eight, implies that they expected, intended, hoped (chose your own word) that it would be read one day. They might have denied this, saying that it was nothing more than a convenient memorandum-book for names and dates, or an amusement which enriched their experience by preserving it. But this begs the question, and it should be pressed; 'Would you', one would like to have asked them, 'be pleased or sorry if, fifty years after your death, someone read it with enjoyment, or even published it?' 'I should hate it'. 'Then why did you not destroy it as you went along, or leave instructions in your Will that it was to be burned?' It is then that the diarist will begin to hedge. And though like Pepys he may keep it in cypher to conceal it from contemporaries (in his case specially from his wife), he is as reluctant to destroy it before his death as to toss the family photograph-albums into the fire.

Some diaries were written deliberately for publication. John Evelyn's was (though he greatly revised it), Greville's, Haydon's, the diary which Dreyfus kept in prison and even Anne Frank's in her horrid garret (we know this, because she often addresses the future reader), and the diaries of great journeys and campaigns like Captain Cook's, Scott's Antarctic journal, Darwin's on the *Beagle*, Lewis and Clark in making the first traverse of North America, Gordon's in Khartoum, and Caulaincourt's during the retreat from Moscow, surely the most dramatic military event of the last two centuries and his diary its most authentic record. Some like Richard Crossman's, which beat all diaries for indiscretion, were written as material for a future book, one of the most rewarding of motives, for it combines freedom of expression with the safeguard of future revision, which thank goodness it never received.

But the norm is the private diary, written with only half an eye cocked on posterity. In it one can weep buckets, as a pagan one can pray, as a believer curse. Some are so intimate that their main purpose is to relieve the mind of deep unhappiness, especially if you are very much alone, or still worse, cannot escape obnoxious company or futile occupation. Listen to Charlotte Brontë at Roe Head school where she was a temporary mistress:

> All this day I have been in a dream, half miserable and half ecstatic . . . I had been toiling for nearly an hour with Miss Lister, Miss Marriott and Ellen Cook, striving to teach them the distinction between an article and a substantive. The parsing lesson was completed; a dead silence had succeeded it in the schoolroom, and I sat sinking from irritation and weariness into a kind of lethargy. The thought came over me, 'Am I to spend all the best part of my

life in this wretched bondage? . . . Must I from day to day sit chained to this chair, prisoned with these four bare walls, while these glorious summer suns are burning in heaven and the year is revolving in its richest glow, and declaring at the end of every summer's day, the time I am losing will never come again?' . . . I felt as if I could have written gloriously. I longed to write. But just then a dolt came up with a lesson, I thought I should have vomited.

This fragment—she kept no regular diary, but it is the very stuff of diaries—was written as a catharsis, and though she could not have known it, she was writing the first draft of the early pages of *Jane Eyre*.

In contrast let me quote a high-spirited diarist who felt little self-reproach and wrote for the sheer enjoyment of writing, Fanny Burney. Here she is being quizzed by George III about her novel *Evelina*:

Coming up close to me, he said, 'But what? What? How was it?'

'Sir?', cried I, not well understanding him.

'How came you—how happened it—what? what?'

'I—I only wrote, sir, for my own amusement—only in some odd, idle hours.'

'But your publishing—your printing—how was that?'

'That was only, sir, only because . . .'

I hesitated most abominably, not knowing how to tell him a long story and growing terribly confused at these questions; besides, to say the truth, his 'What? What?' so reminded me of those vile *Probationary Odes* that in the midst of all my flutter, I was really hardly able to keep my countenance. The *What?* was then repeated with so earnest a look that, forced to say something, I stammeringly answered: 'I thought, sir, it would look very well in print!' . . . He laughed very heartedly—well he might—and walked away to enjoy it, crying out, 'Very fair indeed! That's being very fair and honest!'

Now that's great journalism, in its double sense, an illustration of what a diary should be. You can spot in it the hand of a novelist, but you also know that Miss Burney was recording, as accurately as she could, *how* the king talked. Without her own reactions to this alarming encounter, the passage would lose half its point. It is this give-and-take in her diary, the variety of life seen constantly through the same pair of eyes, which makes it so fresh and spontaneous a document, and she was one of the first to put on record the details of her daily routine which most diarists omit until invited to write it up for the back-page of a colour supplement.

Our present age could be the golden age of diary-keeping. We are less inhibited about what we record; we are all more literate; we know much more about the outside world than our ancestors ever did; we travel more; perhaps we worry more. So let me lay down some laws of diary-keeping. Write it for your children, but don't let them see it till after your death, or until at least fifty years have passed since your youth. This rule, I know, will mean that the diary is not absolute. Just as most people lock the bathroom door against their families, your dairy will omit certain sides of your life, but this does not mean that it will be dishonest. It will be selective. It must not simply record what has happened, but speculate on what is likely to happen. Go easy on the travelogues, for scintillating as the rest of your journal may be, your first impressions of the Parthenon are likely to be as unremarkable as your colour-slides. Avoid the ready-made diary with equal spaces ruled for each day, suggesting that every one is of equal importance. Do not let it become a tyrant demanding a daily meal of fixed quantity. Skip a day or a week occasionally to show that you are master. Be careless, reckless, and enjoy it. Mix public events with the personal. Take a lesson from Creevey. It is interesting to know what the Duke of Wellington said to him on the day after Waterloo, but it becomes more interesting when you discover that Creevey was suffering from violent toothache of which the Duke was wholly unaware. Above all, talk to yourself, 'A genuine diary', write P. A. Spalding, 'must be a dialogue of the self with the self', and he called his book about diaries *Self-Harvest*. That's exactly what a diary is, a daily crop poured into a bin.

There are several reasons why historians should treat diaries with caution. I have already mentioned one of them, the tendency of diarists to self-inflict wounds. Pepys, a great civil servant, and Boswell, the most original of biographers, are often derided for their absurdity because they were too honest in recording their lives, and Lord Rosebery said of Windham's diary, 'He dealt an almost mortal blow to his reputation. We cannot doubt that it would have stood much higher but for his diary.' In contrast, a diarist will often exaggerate his own importance, imagining that conceit and vanity, which he would instantly condemn in another, will escape detection in himself. He will write, 'The Secretary of State was amused when I told him . . .', but he recollects all too well how the Minister was glancing over his shoulder in search of more congenial company. Winston Churchill regarded all diarists with contempt, because 'they give a spurious impression of activity, or, if frank, a damning testimony to their own frailty'. Byron gave up his sporadic journal with the reflection, 'I fear one lies more to oneself than to anyone else. I will keep it no further, to prevent me returning like a dog to the vomit of memory'. Every diary is in part dishonest, if only by omission. One records the day when one gives up smoking, but not the day when one resumes it. Though Evelyn Waugh was candid enough about the debaucheries of his youth, he wrote in his diary next to nothing about the break-up of his first marriage. My father would omit anything which could bring discredit on his closest friends. There is this further hazard for the historian: the diarist may be led by a single compliment or snub to record too flattering or too vituperative an opinion of another person simply because he is still smarting with pleasure or pain. Or like Alan Brooke in his wartime diaries, he is writing at the end of too long a day, and pours into his journal all his pent-up resentment. In none of these cases would the diarist consider that he is engraving a final judgement, and the temptation of the biographer to take it as such must be resisted.

The intimate letter falls into a different category. It has an immediate audience of one. Horace Walpole was one of the few who wrote letters consciously for publication. Though letters gain in readability, they suffer in reliability, from being written primarily not to inform, but to entertain. Ideally, they are continuations of recent conversations, and the best of them, as Dorothy Osborne was the first to discover, are conversational, cajoling, goading, contradicting, exaggerating, affectionate, funny and teasing by turns, with a tone of voice that should echo from the page, with all the hesitations, repetitions and verbal gestures that occur naturally in talk but are rarely reproduced in writing.

Some people have that art—the finest practitioners of it among my own friends were James Pope-Hennessy and Enid Bagnold—and as editor of her letters I found that Virginia Woolf carried it to its most highly developed form. Of course she could be malicious—that was inseparable from her style—revelling in the higher gossip and sometimes the lower, as all Bloomsbury did, trusting that the targets for her wit would remain for ever unaware of it, or if by chance selected passages came to their notice (as of course they always did), that they would laugh it off as affectionate banter, or so she hoped. I often felt the need for some typographical symbol to indicate to the reader and the victim, 'This is a half-truth', 'That is outrageously invented', for her wildest flurries take some beating. Listen to this, for example, from a letter to my mother about Elinor Wylie, the American novelist:

> Oh what an evening! I expected a ravishing and diaphonous dragonfly, a woman who had spirited away four husbands, and wooed from buggery the most obstinate of his adherents; a siren; a green and sweet-voiced nymph. That was what I expected, and came a-tiptoe into the room to find—a solid hunk; a hatchet-minded, cadaverous, acid-voiced, bare-boned, spavined, patriotic, nasal, thick-legged American. All the evening she declaimed unimpeachable truths; and discussed our sales; hers are three times better than mine, naturally; till thank God she began heaving on her chair and made a move as if to go, gracefully yielded to, but not, I beg you to believe, solicited on our parts. Figure my woe, on the stairs, when she murmured, 'It's the other thing I want. Comes of trying to have children. May I go in there?'. So she retired to the WC, emerged refreshed, sent away her cab, and stayed for another hour, hacking us to pieces.

Virginia Woolf's written talk flowed like a stream, now running fast and shallow over pebbles, now with the slow elasticity of a sudden pool. This to Clive Bell, when she was only 26, and was about to embark on her first novel, *The Voyage Out*:

> I think a great deal of my future, and settle what book I am to write—how I shall reform the novel, and capture multitudes of things at present fugitive, enclose the whole, and shape infinite strange shapes. I take a good look at woods in the sunset, and fix men who are breaking stones with an intense gaze, meant to sever them from the past and the future.

Well, that's exactly what she did achieve, but how rarely she communicated these ideas in letters. They were all confided to her diary, and I know of no better illustration of the difference between the two art-forms: her letters were missives tossed like paper darts in a friend's direction to be playfully returned, her diary a receptacle for her ambition, self-appraisal and distress, each a vehicle appropriate to her social or private mood, the diary a hammock, the letter a trampoline. When we put them together, we obtain as complete a picture of a human-being that it is possible to portray outside fiction.

Letters are even less truthful than diaries. We have all written to thank effusively for hospitality that we found less than adequate, or to praise a friend's book which we read with mounting disappointment. Because their prime purpose is to please and amuse, rumour is instantly translated into fact and every event gilded by elaboration. They are less than honest about the writer, less than fair to other people, and like a garden they gain from not being too tightly planned or controlled. They are treacherous sources on which to base biography.

If one is writing the life of someone recently dead, another obstacle intervenes—discretion. One may state nothing but the truth as far as one can discover it, but it is seldom the whole truth. Widows and daughters can fight like tigresses in defence of the reputation of a loved one, as you found, Lord Jenkins, when Lady Violet 'argued a good deal' (as you so gently put it) about your use of Asquith's letters to Venetia Stanley. Living people can be dreadfully hurt by an opinion of them casually expressed fifty years or more ago. My own practice in editing letters and diaries has been to refer to individuals passages that mention them unflatteringly, and ask them how much they would mind publication. My father once wrote of a French journalist, 'She's a fat slug filled with venom. I thought for a moment that she had the grace to blush, but it was only the poison circulating.' When I sent her this passage for approval, she asked me to omit only the word 'fat'. She was a woman of rare generosity.

Where diaries and letters are most useful to a biographer is in gauging how a person, particularly someone eminent in public life, comes to a decision, and how his friendships slowly develop. If fewer diaries are kept, and fewer letters like Asquith's or Neville Chamberlain's to his sister are written, posterity will be the poorer. All we shall be left with is the conclusion of long internal debate, not the process of arriving at it, and we will not be told except in memoirs, which are something quite different, how friends and colleagues reacted to each other in different circumstances.

I have no right to assume that the diary-habit has been abandoned, and Post Office statistics offer no clues as to the content of the mounting volume of the mails. But it is almost certainly true that people are writing fewer personal letters than before. So unusual is it to receive, except from abroad, a letter written for no other reason than to keep in touch, that one tends to ask oneself, 'What does she or he want now?', rapidly skipping to the last paragraph. Even parents and children correspond by telephone.

The telephone—at last I reach it. It is more exciting than the pen. Its ring is more alluring because it is initially anonymous. The telephone's convenience to both parties is immensely seductive, but it leaves no record behind except in fleeting memory or perhaps a scribbled note, and the happy messages recorded by the answering-machine are soon wiped to oblivion. Although the telephone has superseded writing no more than the camera has killed painting, we are inclined more and more to think in terms of sounds and pictures.

Of course for the historian there are compensations. We have more incisive newspapers. We have the cinema, the tape, the video, and soon visual records of House of Commons debates, all of which will provide him with evidence of unprecedented authenticity, revealing as no written record can the gestures, mannerisms, intonations, loaded silences and the very presence of our contemporaries. We can know almost everything there is to know about the first Queen Elizabeth or Cromwell except what it was like to be in the same room with them, but already today's child can witness the precise impact which Churchill made on a vast audience or in animated discussion with Stalin, and both World Wars were filmed with uncompromising brutality. What would we give for the same record of Agincourt! Technology is preserving the oral testimony of people who have played a role in great events, but we should be wary of their evidence if recollected years afterwards in tranquillity. It is often tainted. A man of 70 is not remembering something that occurred when he was 30; he is remembering what he remembered of it when he was 50. His account is polished by repetition, and like any autobiographer, he will make the most of his own part in it.

The upshot is that the more we abandon letter-writing for the telephone, the more we should keep diaries. That word 'keep', which we apply in this sense only to diaries, has a double meaning—that they should be written regularly, and that they should be preserved. This small daily discipline focusses the mind most agreeably, and for writers it is an invaluable method of trying out new literary ideas.

Above all, the diary of a life however humble adds a tessera to the mosaic of recorded history, and like Kilvert's, it may amuse and interest some who come after us.

To Celebrate the Tercentenary of the Glorious Revolution

SIR WILLIAM TEMPLE
AND
ANGLO-DUTCH FRIENDSHIP

SIR RICHARD FABER KCVO CMG FRSL

Read 17 November 1988
Richard Ollard, FRSL, in the Chair

MY TALK this evening is meant as a modest contribution to the William and Mary tercentenary celebrations now in progress. I think I am right in saying that the original idea was to celebrate the Glorious Revolution, as such. Most Englishmen have been taught to regard the events of 1688, like those of 1215, as leading more or less directly to the perfect system of parliamentary democracy with which we are now blessed. But of course there has always been some controversy about the Glorious Revolution, particularly in parts of Scotland and Ireland. There are those who do not think it was glorious and those who do not think that it was really a revolution. So, in the interests of consensus, we are now officially celebrating, not the Glorious Revolution itself, so much as the marriage of William and Mary and their joint accession to the throne. That accession was itself contrived in a spirit of consensus. As has often been said, it was a particularly English sort of fudge, which did its best to disguise the displacement of an annointed —though Roman Catholic—king, by declaring the throne vacant and proposing that it should be filled by his Protestant son-in-law and daughter. William was of course not only James's son-in-law, but also his nephew. Since a prime object of this exercise was to preserve the authority of the Anglican church, and since every effort was made to stick as closely as possible to the old royal line, the Glorious Revolution was arguably more conservative than revolutionary. Perhaps that is why it has always seemed so glorious to the conservative English.

However this may be, there was one aspect of the accession of William and Mary which, with time, has become uncontroversial. It marked the final end of a period of Anglo-Dutch hostility and the beginning of a much longer period, lasting to this day, of predominantly close and friendly relations. It also re-inforced Dutch cultural influence, to our great benefit, especially in banking and in various forms of design. I do not know that this influence was particularly great over our literature, with which of course this Society is mainly concerned. But I have chosen as the subject of my talk this evening a man who contributed as much as any other to the *rapprochement* between Britain and the Netherlands and who was at the same time a distinguished and popular author, as well as an accomplished diplomatist.

Sir William Temple is much less well-known nowadays than he was in his lifetime and in the following century. If you talk about William Temple today, most people will think you mean the twentieth-century Archbishop of Canterbury. In my view Sir William has been cast into a deeper oblivion than he deserves. Besides negotiating the Triple Alliance of 1668 with the Netherlands and Sweden—a diplomatic *coup* which was famous in its day—he wrote a number of celebrated Essays, perhaps more cultivated than scholarly, but full of imagination and originality. He was also master of an elegant, yet straightforward, style that helped to form eighteenth-century English. Dr Johnson was a great admirer of this style, although it was much lighter than his own, and described Temple as the first writer to give cadence to English prose. Others have described him as the first writer of political memoirs in English, though that may seem rather less of a recommendation.

When young, Temple was the lover, and later the husband, of Dorothy Osborne; when old, he was for several years the patron and employer of the young Jonathan Swift. He was a keen gardener, who introduced varieties of fruit into England and helped to create a more natural taste in garden design. More to the point this evening, he played a considerable part, as Ambassador at The Hague, in bringing about the marriage of William and Mary. In April 1676 William broached with Temple privately the possibility of such a marriage. They talked for two hours, both about the political and the personal aspects of the match, and with Temple's encouragement the Prince decided to go ahead. In the light of 1688 it is ironical that English politicians opposed to the Court should have advised William secretely not to compromise himself by marrying James's daughter. Danby, then Charles II's chief Minister, noted on Temple's letter of the 23rd of April reporting his talk with the Prince that 'this was the first Motion in that Affair'.

Temple died at the end of the seventeenth century, but his reputation still stood high for several decades. The famous Lord Chesterfield, who was himself Ambassador at The Hague from 1728 to 1732, seems to have liked to feel that, in his close relations with Dutch officials, he was following Temple's example. In 1740 Chesterfield's most intimate friend, the Earl of Scarborough, committed suicide, after resigning from the Ministry. I cannot resist quoting what Dr Maty, Chesterfield's biographer, has to say about this tragic, though decorously Augustan incident, since it illustrates the esteem in which Temple's writings were then held. According to Maty, on the morning of Scarborough's suicide:

> he paid a long visit to Lord Chesterfield, and opened himself to him with great earnestness on many subjects. As he appeared somewhat discomposed, his friend pressed him in vain to stay and dine with him; which he refused, but most tenderly embraced him at parting. It happened in the course of the conversation that something was spoken of which related to Sir William Temple's negotiations, when the two friends not agreeing about the circumstances, Lord Chesterfield, whose memory was at all times remarkably good, referred Lord Scarborough to the page of Sir William's memoirs where the matter was mentioned. After his lordship's death the book was found open at that very page. Thus he seems, in his last moments, to have been still attentive to his friend, and desirous that he should know that he was so.

I cannot go in any detail this evening into Temple's life, character or career. What I want to talk about chiefly is the book that he wrote about the Netherlands in 1672 and how this contributed to Anglo-Dutch friendship. But first I must recall briefly his work as a diplomatist, as well as a writer, and try to set it against the immediate historical background. That background was, of course, not one of friendship between the two countries, but of envy and hostility. It is true that, in the latter part of Elizabeth I's reign, the English had helped the Dutch in their struggle against Spain, if not quite as effectively as they liked to think. But, in the seventeenth century, relations between these two maritime and mainly Protestant countries had worsened. This was largely due to trade rivalry, all over the world, as well as to disputes about the freedom of the seas, invoked by the English in the Dutch-dominated tropics and by the Dutch in what the English regarded as their home waters.

These naval and commercial disputes were, from time to time, envenomed by more or less ideological differences. England was still basically a monarchical country, as well as an aristocratic one. Holland, the leading province of The Netherlands, was predominantly under the control of a republican elite, of merchants and their descendants, normally known as 'patricians' and regarded by English diehards as not being fully gentlemen in their understanding of the word. On top of this the English resented being beaten to the post by a smaller, and more recent, country which had owed something (if less than they liked to think) to their intervention. To this period largely belong the derogatory English phrases, still to some extent current, about double Dutch, Dutch courage, Dutch treats, Dutch bargains and Dutch uncles. None of our other neighbours, not even the French, seem to have put so many homely insults of this kind into common English usage.

It is fair to say that, by the middle of the seventeenth century, the Netherlands had largely replaced Spain as our national enemy, at least in commercial circles. Three naval wars, the first under Cromwell and two others under Charles II, reflected this enmity. There were ups and downs in all of them; but on the whole the English had the upper hand in the first, and in most of the pitched naval battles, while the Dutch were able to put the English at a disadvantage by the end of the second and third wars. The second war, indeed, closed in a great national humiliation for England, when the Dutch fleet sailed up the Medway. This was one reason why the third war was launched, although popular feeling against the Dutch had begun to subside since the fifties and early sixties.

Charles II had been personally reluctant to engage in the Second Dutch War, but was largely responsible for the Third. He wanted to wipe out the Medway humiliation. More important his difficulties with Parliament, and his need for money, had made him adopt —though not always openly—a policy of co-operation with France which almost inevitably involved conflict with the Netherlands. He was of course a grandchild of France himself—his mother being a daughter of Henri Quatre—and, like most European rulers at the time (including the leading Dutch patricians) had considerable admiration for Louis XIV's methods and achievements. He would have been glad to be able to exercise such apparently untrammelled authority in England. The Dutch leaders were themselves extremely anxious for good relations with the French, who had been their allies in the second Dutch War. But they did not want to have them as their immediate neighbours. It was the object of all three countries (France, England and the Netherlands) not to find themselves isolated against a combination of the other two. That nevertheless had happened to England in the second Dutch War and was to happen to the Netherlands in the third.

Temple, serving in a Brussels still under Spanish rule, had been patriotically anti-Dutch while the second Dutch War was in progress; but soon afterwards he became increasingly alarmed by the French threat to the Spanish Low Countries. He saw clearly that it could not be to England's advantage to have all her closest neighbours under French control or influence. So he was enthusiastic, when—though for largely tactical reasons and in order to increase his bargaining power with the French—Charles II determined at the beginning of 1668 on what seemed a totally new policy. The King sent Temple to The Hague to negotiate a defensive alliance with the Dutch as well as an agreement to promote a peace between France and Spain that would prevent further French advances in Flanders. With the adherence of Sweden this negotiation became the famous Triple Alliance. It was as much a reversal of policy for the Dutch as for the English; but, initially at least, it was popular in both countries, because of the fear of French expansion and the dread that this in turn would promote the cause of Roman Catholicism. Pepys noted in his diary at the end of January 'the good news of our making a league now with Holland against the French coming over them or us'. Three days later he added that the league 'pleases everybody and they say vexes France'.

However, the practical effect of the Triple Alliance was short-lived, because Charles II went on to conclude the Secret Treaty of Dover with the French and then, as promised in this Treaty, launched the

Third Dutch War. While this further reversal of policy was being planned Temple remained at The Hague, receiving periodical assurances that there had been no change of heart in Whitehall. These assurances came from men who, like Temple himself, were kept in the dark; only two of Charles's Ministers, Clifford and Arlington, were originally party to the King's secret policy.

Temple had nevertheless had some suspicions, even in the first honeymoon of the Triple Alliance, and was only too aware that a new, chilly, wind was beginning to blow. It was not a good sign that he was being bombarded with commercial complaints from the City, or that the Dutch were beginning to have their own doubts about English steadiness. In a despatch home in April 1669, now in the Public Record Office, he wrote:

> For my owne opinion it is freely this, that if wee thinke wee cannot find very well consisting measures with the Dutch, and can finde them better and safer with the French, wee should take them but bee sure of them before we threaten it heere.

Temple himself was of course convinced that the right policy was still, in his own words, to 'hinder the growing exorbitant power of France'. But he knew that he was regarded as being too pro-Dutch in London and he could not afford to seem lacking a proper sense of British interests. In the same month the Dutch Grand Pensionary, Johan de Witt, examined him closely about the allegations of a Swedish agent that the French had corrupted English Ministers and had obtained the reversal of the Triple Alliance policy. Temple found it increasingly difficult to parry such enquiries, though he knew that there had been no change in his instructions, or in his own attitude.

Finally, at the end of 1670, Temple was recalled from The Hague, to find a cool reception in Whitehall very different from what he had experienced just after the signature of the Triple Alliance. Arlington, who was virtually Foreign Secretary and had been his patron and personal friend, kept him waiting for an hour and a half in an outer room; when he was finally received, Temple was given no explanation of his recall. The King was equally, though less unpleasantly, evasive at a meeting in The Mall.

Temple, who was thin-skinned and nothing if not perceptive, soon realised that he was not wanted at Court. He had a brush with the Roman Catholic Clifford, who wanted him to go back to The Hague and put the Dutch in the wrong. Temple declined to do this, saying heatedly that he would 'speak of all Men what I thought of them'. He decided it was time to retire to the discreet security of his country house at Sheen, where he remained unemployed, though not inactive, until the end of 1673. By that time Charles, conscious of the costs of the Third Dutch War and ceding to public and parliamentary pressure, had resolved to seek a separate peace with the Dutch. Temple was accordingly brought back into favour and business, so that he could negotiate terms through the Spanish Ambassador at London. He managed this with his usual rapidity and persuasiveness and was then sent back to The Hague as Ambassador, remaining there, or at the Conference of Nijmegen, until he was recalled for good in early 1679.

During this second period in the Netherlands perhaps Temple's chief contribution to Anglo-Dutch relations was his personal friendship with William III, who had outgrown his minority and restored the influence of the House of Orange over his countrymen. Temple was twenty-two years older than William; but the two men much respected each other. The Ambassador had an access to the Prince that most modern Ambassadors would envy; according to Temple's sister, William being 'fond of speaking English . . . and of eating their plain way' would habitually take two or three meals a week in their house when he was at The Hague. I have already mentioned the part Temple played in bringing about the marriage of William and Mary. It was Charles who in the end decided in favour of this match. His brother James, to whom the marriage was eventually to prove fatal, only accepted the decision with some reluctance, saying of the King: 'I would be glad if all his subjects would learn of me to obey Him'. The accession of William and Mary, often represented as a triumph for Parliament, could never have come about without this assertion, and acceptance, of royal authority.

Temple, like many others, had had the idea of such a marriage in mind well before William broached it with him in 1676. He had already reported to the Prince that, when he had kissed hands before leaving for Holland, James (then Duke of York) had told him:

> That he lookt upon your Highness's Interests, as the same with the King's and his own; and that if there were any Thing wherein you could use his Service, you might be sure of it. I replyed, Pray, Sir, remember, there is nothing you except, and you do not know how far a young Prince's Desire may go; but I am resolved to tell Him what you say, and, if there be Occasion, to be a witness of it: The

Duke smiled, Well, well, you may tell him what I bid you. Upon which I said, At least I will tell the Prince that you smiled when I told you so, which, I am sure, is a great deal better than if you had frowned.

Temple, who always described himself as a 'legal Man', was in retirement by 1688 and does not seem to have played any part in the Revolution. He declined office under William III, though his son was made Secretary for War and he himself was ready with advice when William asked for it. He also published a short *Introduction to the History of England* in 1695, which drew an implicit parallel between the careers and characters of William I and William III. The purpose of this was to reconcile Englishmen to having a Dutch stadholder as king, by stressing the advantages that a continental dimension had in both cases brought to England. In a passage about the Conqueror's Norman favourites he went out of his way to explain, and to excuse, William III's Dutch friends, like Portland and Albemarle.

But perhaps nothing that Temple did had so much significance for Anglo-Dutch relations as the book that he wrote during his temporary retirement in 1672. Entitled *Observations upon the United Provinces of the Netherlands*, this is the only one of Temple's works currently in print. It was published in the Spring of 1673 and the first edition was almost immediately followed by a second. A Dutch translation came out in the same year and a French translation in 1680.

At home there had been four editions by 1686, when Bishop Burnet described it as 'the perfectest book of its kind that is perhaps in being'. That tribute, which led to renewed sales, was all the more convincing, because Burnet was by no means an uncritical admirer of Temple. He recognised that Sir William had 'a true judgment in affairs'; but he regarded him as 'a vain man, much blown up in his own conceit, which he shewed too indecently on all occasions'. From his standpoint of liberal Anglicanism Burnet condemned Temple as an Epicurean, who thought that 'religion was fit only for the mob' and that 'things were as they are from all eternity'; an admirer of the Chinese Confucians; 'a corrupter of all that came near him'; and a devotee of 'study, ease and pleasure'. There was some truth, though more exaggeration, in all these judgements.

The *Observations* begin with a historical sketch of the development of the United Provinces up to the beginning of the seventeenth century. They continue with descriptions of The Provinces' political constitution, of their topographical situation, of the character of the people, of their religion, of their trade and of their forces and revenues. The book ends with a chapter on 'The Causes of their Fall in 1672'. I shall come back to this in a moment.

Perhaps the most remarkable thing about this slim, yet highly intelligent survey is that, though the tone is cool rather than hotly partisan, it gives a respectful and sympathetic account of the Netherlands at a time of Anglo-Dutch war. Of course war between European countries was not such a total experience in the seventeenth century as it has been in this. But even a tithe of Temple's respect and sympathy for the Dutch and their government would have been difficult to conceive in a publication about Germany by a former British official during the Second World War. That Temple could take this risk of being thought unpatriotic is an indication that feeling in England as a whole was no longer so anti-Dutch as it had been; it is also a tribute to his own courage and skill.

The decline in hostility was no doubt due to increasing English commercial success, in various parts of the world, as well as to the growing fear of France and Roman Catholicism; it must also have been affected by the evident popularity of the short-lived Triple Alliance. Temple himself could claim that, during the Third Dutch War, the people were not angry against the Dutch in the way that they had been during the Second. In his book he argued that his fellow-countrymen were too ignorant of 'a Countrey so much in our eye, the common road of our travels, as well as subject of our talk; and which we have been of late not only curious, but concerned to know'. At the same time he took the precaution of adopting a balanced tone, which would avoid any charge of personal bias. He inserted a glowing account of the achievements of the Royal Navy in the Second Dutch War, in spite of the ravages of Plague and Fire in London: two naval victories, the third battle undecided, but one in which, as the Dutch Grand Pensionary had said to Temple, 'we gain'd more Honour to our Nation, and to the invincible courage of our Sea-Men than by the other Two Victories'. All this was designed to make English readers feel good. So was Temple's belief that Dutch trade had passed its meridian.

Finally Temple's emphasis on the fall of the Dutch patrician regime in 1672, as a result of its initial inability to withstand the French land invasion, allowed him to suggest that, since the Netherlands could no longer be a threat to Britain, he was writing for the curious, as an idle man, rather than as a politician with a message and a policy to put across. This was typical of his disarming tactics and ought not to be taken too strictly at face value. He went on to put the case for the Triple Alliance as strongly as he could, claiming with perhaps pardonable exaggeration:

By an Alliance with this State in January 68 (which was received with incredible Joy and Applause among them) His Majesty became the unquestioned Arbiter of all the Affairs of Christendom; Made a Peace between the two great Crowns [of France and Spain], at Aix la Chapelle, which was avowed by all the World to be perfectly His Own; And was received with equal Applause of Christian Princes abroad, and of his Subjects at home; And for three years succeeding, by the unshaken Alliance and Dependence of the United States His Majesty remained Absolute Master of the Peace of Christendom, and in a posture of giving Bounds to the greatest, as well as Protection to the weakest of his Neighbours.

It is difficult not to conclude that, in spite of what he called the Fall of the United Provinces (or 'United States') in 1672, Temple was trying to prepare the ground for a resumption of the Triple Alliance policy. We know from his correspondence with the Earl of Essex that, while he chose to describe himself in 1672 as completely buried in the country, by August of 1673 he was meeting politicians and keenly following current affairs.

In the interest of renewed Anglo-Dutch alliance Temple needed not only to make the Netherlands respectable, but to counter the view that England would benefit from their destruction. With the first aim in mind he reassured his Restoration readers that the government of the United Provinces was not 'a Popular Government, as it is generally esteemed by those who passing or living in these Countreys, content themselves with common Observations and Inquiries'; in reality, he said, it was 'a sort of Oligarchy'. The members of this oligarchy were expressly educated 'for the service of their Countrey in the Magistracy of their Towns, their Provinces, and their State'; in most cases they came from families who had been similarly educated and employed 'for many years, and some for several Ages'. Thus they were 'not men of mean or Mechanick Trades, as it is commonly received among Foreigners, and makes the subject of Comical Jests upon their Government'.

Temple thought that the vast growth in Dutch trade and riches could be explained by the prevailing industry and parsimony, by a long period of civil peace and by the mighty increase of population in a small space. This confluence of people had in turn been promoted by wars in surrounding countries, by the financial security offered by the Bank of Amsterdam and by the general liberty of conscience allowed to immigrants. Coming to this last point Temple abandoned his pose of scientific detachment and came out unmistakably, and eloquently, in favour. He declaimed, with almost lyrical fervour:

But in this Commonwealth, no man having any reason to complain of oppression in Conscience; and no man having hopes by advancing his Religion, to form a Party, or break in upon the State, the differences in Opinion make none in Affections, and little in Conversation, where it serves but for entertainment and variety. They argue without interest or anger; They differ without enmity or scorn. And they agree without confederacy. Men live together like Citizens of the world, associated by the common ties of Humanity and by the bonds of Peace, Under the impartial protection of indifferent Laws, with equal encouragement of all Art and Industry, and equal freedom of Speculation and Enquiry; All men enjoying their imaginary excellencies and acquisitions of knowledg, with as much safety, as their more real possessions and improvements of Fortune. The power of Religion among them, where it is, lies in every man's heart; The appearance of it, is but like a piece of Humanity, by which every one falls most into the company or conversation of those whose Customs and Humours, whose Talk and Disposition they like best: And as in other places, 'tis in every man's choice, with whom he will eat or lodg, with whom go to Market, or to Court; So it seems to be here, with whom he will pray or go to Church, or associate in the Service and worship of God; Nor is any more notice taken, or more censure past, of what every one choses in these cases, than in the other.

Temple pays other warm tributes to Dutch civilisation, particularly to the beauty and cleanliness of the towns and houses. He is less complimentary about the climate. Later in life he believed that his own health had been permanently damaged by the moist atmosphere and keen winds; he found the Dutch Spring shorter, the Winter colder and some parts of the Summer hotter than in England. But this is one of the few aspects of life in Holland where he sounds at all reproachful.

Replying to those who argued that England would benefit from Dutch ruin, Temple made a number of points. One argument sometimes put forward was that, if Dutch trade were damaged as a result of foreign intervention, it 'would of course fall to our share in England'. Temple countered that it would 'break into several pieces, and shift either to us, to Flanders, to the Hans-Towns, or any other parts, according as the most of those circumstances should any where concur to invite it . . . as appears to have formerly drawn it into Holland'. Another argument was that, if the Netherlands were reduced to great extremities, they 'would chuse our Subjection rather than any other'. Temple disputed this; he thought that, in such a crisis, they would be more likely to revert to the Hapsburg Empire. He also denied that, if the Prince of Orange were made sovereign, though by foreign arms, he 'would be a great Prince'. On the contrary, he maintained, 'those Provinces would soon become a very mean Countrey'; the use of force would raise discontent and sedition; 'The People would scatter, Industry would faint, Banks would dissolve, And Trade would decay . . .' Throughout this discussion Temple was able to turn his experience and knowledge as a diplomatist to good account as an author.

I should like to end with a slightly closer look at what Temple had to say in his chapter about the Dutch 'People and Dispositions'. Here he keeps a particularly careful balance and seems to be at his most detached. He finds much to like and admire; but, where he has reservations, he expresses them.

I have already stressed that Temple was writing in time of war. Even if he had not been, his professional formation as a diplomatist would probably have guarded him from excessive enthusiasm. A diplomatist abroad can hardly succeed in his job without some liking for, or at least some understanding of, his host country. But he is unlikely to carry much weight at home if he seems to have become a total convert to foreign virtues. In any case the rather detached and observant attitudes that diplomatists are obliged to cultivate, as they try to interpret two countries to each other, induce a habit of detachment which tends in time to colour most of their thoughts and feelings.

More generally, as I have tried to show, the seventeenth century was a time when English prejudices against the Dutch were stronger than they have usually been. It has often been noted since then how well most Dutch and English people get on together, when they are not fighting each other. There seems to be some temperamental sympathy, perhaps originating in a sort of racial affinity. The English and Dutch languages have a number of words in common, while many of our Anglo-Saxon ancestors are believed to have broken their journies to this island, for long periods, along the northern shores of the Netherlands. But of course this temperamental sympathy, whatever its origin, has not prevented the two peoples from criticising each other from time to time. The Dutch have sometimes found the English too stiff or too ostentatious; the English have sometimes found the Dutch a bit solemn and heavy-going. This is partly because Dutch society as a whole has been in the past still more Puritanical than English society—or at least with less of a Cavalier leaven in it. But it is also because relatively few Englishmen have ever been able to speak Dutch fluently, so that conversation between the two peoples has largely been in French or, more often nowadays, in English. If it is difficult to be entertaining in one's own language, it is still more difficult in another.

Temple seems to have been able to read Dutch; but we do not know how often, or how well, he spoke it. He could converse fluently in French and Spanish and probably used these languages with those of his diplomatic and official acquaintances who could not speak English. He records some talks he had had with less educated Dutchmen on his travels round the country. Perhaps he spoke enough Dutch for that, or perhaps it was mainly people with a smattering of English who sought him out. At any rate he shared some of the usual English preconceptions about Dutch character. Himself a lively and imaginative talker, he found that conversation in Holland tended to run too exclusively on business. This was certainly not because the Dutch lacked intelligence or ability: 'though these people, who are naturally Cold and Heavy', he wrote, 'may not be ingenious enough to furnish a pleasant or agreeable Conversation, yet they want not plain down-right sense to understand and do their business both publique and private, which is a Talent very different from the other; and I know not whether they often meet . . .'

Another deficiency which Temple thought he detected in the Dutch was a lack of warm and romantic feeling. He had himself been almost excessively romantic as a young man, during his long and passionate courtship of Dorothy Osborne; this had been kept at fever pitch by their joint taste for the highly-flown, heroic, romances of the period before the Restoration brought in satire and cynicism. So it is not surprising that he observed of Holland:

> In general, All Appetites and Passions seem to run cooler here, than in other Countreys where I have converst . . . Their Tempers are not aiery enough for Joy, or any unusual strains of pleasant Humour; nor warm enough for love. This is talkt of sometimes among the younger men, but as a thing they have heard of, rather than felt; and as a discourse that becomes them, rather than affects them. I have known some among them that personated Lovers well enough but none that I ever thought were at heart in love; Nor any of the Women that seem'd at all to care whether they were so or no.

Perhaps, Temple speculated, the phlegmatic behaviour of the Dutch was due to 'the dulness of their Air', or perhaps to their preoccupation with business, or perhaps to their being 'such lovers of their Liberty, as not to bear the servitude of a Mistris any more than that of a Master'.

This is as far as Temple goes in his criticisms. On the credit side he particularly praises the probity of the Dutch, their frugality, their industry and steadiness, their charity and their readiness to contribute to handsome public works.

Temple divides the people into five classes: 'The Clowns or Boors . . . who cultivate the land. The Mariners or Schippers, who supply their Ships and Inland-Boats. The Merchants or Traders, who fill their Towns. The Renteneers, or men that live in all their chief Cities upon the Rents or Interest of Estates formerly acquired in their Families; And the Gentlemen and Officers of their Armies'.

He describes the first, peasant, class as 'a Race of people diligent rather than laborious; dull and slow of understanding and so not dealt with by hasty words, but managed easily by soft and fair; and yeelding to plain Reason, if you give them time to understand it. In the Countrey and Villages not too near the great Towns, they seem plain and honest, and content with their own . . .'

The second class, or seamen, 'are a plain but much rougher people', he writes, 'whether from the Element they live in, or from their Food, which is generally Fish and Corn and heartier than that of the Boors'.

The third class, of town-dwelling merchants and artisans, 'Are more Mercurial . . . of mighty Industry and constant application to the Ends they propose and pursue. They make use of their Skill and their Wit, to take advantage of other Men's Ignorance and Folly they deal with: Are great Exacters where the Law is in their own hands. In other points, where they deal with men that understand like themselves, and are under the reach of Justice and Laws, they are the plainest and best dealers in the world . . .'

As to the fourth class, the patrician *rentiers*, they are like the third class in modesty of dress and behaviour and in 'Parsimony of living'; but they are much better educated, particularly in civil law, so as to fit them for their public role as magistrates.

Finally the Gentlemen or Nobles are very few in the province of Holland, 'most of the Families having been extinguished in the long wars with Spain'. Such as remain are almost all employed in the Army or in the public service. They are a good deal different from the rest of the people and tend to imitate the French too much. But otherwise, in Temple's experience, they are 'an Honest, Well-natur'd, Friendly, and Gentlemanly sort of men, and acquit themselves generally with Honour and Merit, where their Countrey employs them'.

Parts of this analysis, summary as it is, could still be applied today. Of course Dutch society has become much more complex; the patricians no longer monopolise government; there is a new class of industrial workers; and the lines between all the classes are less sharply drawn. Subject to these many changes, there is still some truth in what he writes in this chapter, notably in the final paragraph in which he sums up his impressions. That paragraph is a beautiful and well-known piece of English prose, which shows his style at its most balanced and cadenced. It is also a brief description of the country that would still be recognisable to foreigners, even though they might prefer to have it worded more warmly. It is a short paragraph and I should like to quote it in full:

To conclude this Chapter: Holland is a Countrey where the Earth is better than the Air, and Profit more in request than Honour; where there is more Sense than Wit; More good Nature than good Humour; And more Wealth than Pleasure; Where a man would chuse rather to travel, than to live; Shall find more things to observe than desire; And more persons to esteem than to love. But the same Qualities and Dispositions do not value a private man and a State, nor make a Conversation agreeable, and a Government great. Nor is it unlikely that some very great King might make but a very ordinary private Gentleman, and some very extraordinary Gentleman might be capable of making but a very mean Prince.

When he wrote that foreigners would find more Dutchmen to esteem than to love, Temple may have been comparing The Hague with Brussels where, as a younger man, he seems to have been popular with both sexes. The phrase also mirrored his personal feelings about Charles II and William of Orange. He almost certainly esteemed William more highly than Charles; but Charles had more charm and Temple habitually wrote about him with deeper affection.

It is of course impossible to quantify the effect of a single book in moulding public opinion. There were other studies of the United Provinces available to late seventeenth-century English readers. But Bishop Burnet was not the only critic to regard Temple's as the best—and it must surely have been the most agreeably written. It was certainly widely read, since it was well-timed to meet a growing wish for better Anglo-Dutch relations. Charles II was still reluctant to make an enemy of France, and was still angling for French subsidies; but the Third Dutch War had persuaded him that he could not afford, and would not benefit from, further attempts to wreak vengeance on the Dutch. Fears of French expansion continued to spread in the country at large; even the future James II at one time suspected that Louis XIV was aiming at a 'universal monarchy'. In any case popular antipathy to the prospect of a Roman Catholic dynasty in England was bound to increase William III's chances of eventually acceding to the English and Scottish thrones.

Temple had once assured James II, when the latter was still Duke of York, that he 'would always follow the Crown as became me; nor could any Thing make the least Scruple in this Resolution, unless Things should ever grow so desperate as to bring in Foreigners'. He did not of course regard the Prince of Orange as a foreigner in this sense. In 1680, well before Charles II's death, he urged the Prince privately to consider whether he should come over and try to persuade the King to accept his brother's exclusion from the throne. In the previous year he had been anxious that the Prince should improve his own claim by fathering a male heir. He told Henry Sidney, his successor at The Hague, that there was nothing for the Prince to do 'but to get a boy'; apparently he even supplied him with a recipe for the purpose. (What sort of recipe we are not told; it cannot have had a very high success rate.)

On the whole it seems clear that, since the signature of the Triple Alliance, if not before, Temple consistently supported a policy of Anglo-Dutch alliance and of resistance to French aggrandisement. He advised Henry Sidney 'not to mistrust Holland in their trade, commerce, or anything else, for he was sure we should find a faithful alliance there'. Personally he was less worried than many Englishmen by the idea of having a Roman Catholic King; but he thought that, in the long term, the country would only unite behind the sort of policies he advocated if it was governed by a Protestant dynasty. So, in spite of his personal loyalty, first to Charles II and later to James II, and in spite of his conservative temperament, he helped to pave the way for William III's accession. His book on the United Provinces certainly contributed towards this general change in national direction. So did his public career and his private influence.

Although I set out to celebrate Temple as an author, I seem to have spent rather more time recalling him as a man of affairs. After the success of his *Observations upon the United Provinces* he went on to write, and publish, a number of other essays and memoirs. Parts of the essays deserve a permanent place in any collection of English prose. But I suppose it is true to say that his attitude to authorship remained throughout that of a gentlemanly amateur; in the *Last Essays of Elia* Charles Lamb cited him as a model of the genteel, or gentlemanly, style. Not that this elegant amateurishness prevented Temple from taking seriously what he wrote, or from expecting and wanting it to be admired. There is at least as much affectation as candour in the deprecating remarks with which he introduced the *Observations*:

> I am very sensible', he confessed, 'how ill a Trade it is to write, where much is ventur'd, and little can be gain'd; since whoever does it ill, is sure of contempt, and the justliest that can be, when no man provokes him to discover his own follies, or to trouble the world. If he writes well, he raises the envy of those Wits that are possest of the Vogue, and are jealous of their Preferment there, as if it were in Love, or in State; And have found, that the nearest way to their own Reputation, lyes right, or wrong, by the derision of other men. But however I am not in pain: for 'tis the affectation of Praise, that makes the fear of Reproach; And I write without other design than of entertaining very idle men, and among them my self.

Yet this amateur author, who claimed to be indifferent to praise, was certainly not indifferent to criticism. Similarly, for all his supposed idleness, he was busy enough to anticipate the Anglo-Dutch alliance against French ambition that was to dominate British foreign policy for a quarter of a century.

Katja Reissner Memorial Lecture

THOMAS CRANMER, THE PRAYER BOOK AND THE ENGLISH LANGUAGE

REVEREND DR VIVIAN GREEN

Read 23 November 1989
Miss P. D. James, OBE, JP, FRSL, in the Chair

THOMAS CRANMER, the quincentenary of whose birth occurs this year, was without doubt one of the major architects of the English language, even if there may be differences of opinion as to how exactly he should be ranked in that respect. Hilaire Belloc, who surely was no friend to Anglicanism, declared that Cranmer 'was of that small band, standing out as isolated figures far separated down the ages, who have the gift of speech . . . who serve the Muses and the leader of their choir, the God of the Silver Bow . . . Cranmer constructs with a success only parallelled by the sonnets of Shakespeare.' With more measured tread and a less rhetorical flourish C. S. Lewis conceded that Cranmer wrote a 'prose with which it is difficult to find any fault' but he added 'it gives curiously little pleasure . . . It is praiseworthy: it is (if I may put it in that way) devastatingly praiseworthy.' This is really almost to condemn with faint praise. We will this afternoon try to enquire as to what may be the likely verdict on Cranmer's writing, seeking to ascertain what he actually wrote, not in itself an easy matter, and to measure his future influence.

Cranmer was a man well on in his years by Tudor standards, 55 years old, when he made his first major contribution to the English liturgy. Behind him there lay a wealth of experience in the explosive Tudor world, and latterly the dangerous and treacherous Tudor court. When he was 14 years old he had gone to the recently founded Jesus College in Cambridge where he was, his later secretary Morice said, 'nosselled in the grossest kynd of sophistry.' But he was certainly subject to other intellectual and religious influences during his twenty years at Cambridge. Whether or not he actually went to the lectures which Erasmus was delivering there in 1511 we do not know but he must have absorbed something of the 'new divinity' associated with Erasmus and would have been aware of Erasmus's belief that the Bible should be studied in its original languages and very conceivably of his approval of the vernacular. There had been a brief interruption to his career for before his ordination he had married a local girl, Joan, possibly the daughter of the landlord of the Dolphin Inn in Bridge Street, but she died in childbirth and Cranmer was re-elected to his fellowship which he was to hold for another fourteen years. He held no important post in the university but his growing reputation as a scholar was such that he was one of those invited to staff Cardinal Wolsey's intended new foundation at Oxford and only refused the invitation at the last minute. He was also one of those associated with the group of Lutheran sympathizers who used to meet at the White Horse Inn. The Cambridge experience, if in some ways hidden from our view, was unquestionably the major influence in Cranmer's life, for above all else he was and remained a scholar and a don. His devotion to learning was paramount.

Then chance, fate, call it what you will made a decisive intervention in Cranmer's life. He was asked to act as a tutor to the sons of the Cressy family, a family to which on his mother's side he was distantly related, at Waltham. On a second visit there he found staying in the house two of Henry VIII's ministers, for the king was hunting in the neighbourhood, Stephen Gardiner and Edward Fox. Not unnaturally at some stage the conversation turned on the king's great affair, his attempt to divorce Catherine of Aragon. Cranmer apparently suggested that it would be good sense to consult the theologians of the universities. Although it was not a novel suggestion, Cranmer's unfeigned support of the king won his hearers' attention. When Henry learned of his readiness to write in favour of the divorce, he was sent to reside at Durham House, the London residence of the Boleyn family in the Strand where, we are told 'from scripture and old authors' he composed arguments in favour of the divorce.

He found himself appointed to the embassy which Anne Boleyn's father, the Earl of Wiltshire, was to lead to Italy in 1530; and it is probable that his experience of Rome may have strengthened further his incipient Protestantism. Then he was himself appointed to head an embassy to the Emperor Charles V, Catherine of Aragon's nephew. While the embassy seemed outwardly fruitless, it had for Cranmer some important by-products, for he made his first real contacts with the German Lutherans and in 1532 married the niece of one of them. Margaret the niece of Andreas Osiander of Nuremberg. It was moreover at Nuremberg, which was a Protestant city that he went, as his predecessor as ambassador Sir Thomas Elyot told the duke of Norfolk, on a Sunday in Lent to a Lutheran service where the epistle and gospel were read in the vernacular. 'Mr Cranmer', Sir Thomas Elyot who was not himself in favour of the new service told his correspondent, 'sayith it was shewed to him that in the Epistle and Gospel thei kept not the ordre that we doo, but doo peruse every day one chapitre of the New Testament.' Here probably was Cranmer's first experience of hearing any part of a religious service in the vernacular, and the seed once planted was to grow slowly but surely and bear fruit.

His marriage to Margaret Osiander, for which there is no explicit contemporary evidence, showed equally that he had already absorbed and was ready to practise radical Protestant ideas, for his marriage constituted a fundamental and deliberate breach of church order unless we suppose that, like his master, he had allowed his grosser instincts to circumscribe his reasonable judgement, which seems unlikely.

Henry was so well pleased with his ambassador, clever, scholarly, devout and suitably sychophantic, that after pondering the matter for some time he decided to appoint Cranmer archbishop of Canterbury in succession to the octogenarian William Warham who had died five months earlier.

With Cranmer's part in the royal affair and its sequel, the breach with Rome and the slow and fluctuating process of Protestantization we are, I think, only concerned in so far as it affected the introduction of English as a medium for worship. For Thomas Cranmer as for the king's vice-gerent Thomas Cromwell the basic authority for the Church and for the royal supremacy to which they both so strongly adhered was the Word of God in the Scriptures; sola scriptura. This was the corrosive which would explode the false teachings of Rome. It was therefore in the first instance the instrument by which true Christian teaching and doctrine could be communicated to the faithful in their own tongue, so that, in the words of Erasmus 'the countryman might sing them at his plough, the weaver chant them at his loom, the traveller beguile with them the tedium of his journey.' 'Saint Jerome' as William Tyndale whose version of the New Testament in English was published in 1526,' also translated the Bible into his mother tongue. Why may not we also?' In 1534 Convocation besought the king to authorize an official translation of the Bible. Three years later a version attributed to Thomas Matthew appeared. It was not a new version but a combination of Tyndale's translation of the Pentateuch and of the New Testament and Coverdale's translation of the Old Testament which had appeared in 1535. Cranmer greatly approved and asked Cromwell to show it to the king and get 'if you can, a licence that the same may be sold and read of every person . . . until such time that the bishops shall set forth a better translation, which I think will not be till a day after doomsday.' As a result a licence was granted and Coverdale was commissioned to revise the text which was published in 1539 and was known as the Great Bible, of which seven editions were made before December 1541. A royal injunction ordered that a copy of the Bible in English should be placed in every church.

To the second edition of 1540 Cranmer contributed a preface, so that the bible is sometimes known, though incorrectly, as Cranmer's Bible. In some sense he wrote at an unfortunate time as it coincided with a flurry of reaction on Henry VIII's part which made the king averse to the reading of the English Bible by every Tom, Dick or Harry, so that Cranmer thought it proper to urge that the English Bible should not be read unadvisedly 'for truly some there are that be too slow and need the spur; some other seem too quick, and need more of the bridle.' Yet in his preface he made plain the 'largeness and utility of the scripture', 'how it containeth fruitful instruction and erudition for every man . . . In the Scriptures be the fat pastures of the soul; therein is no venemous meat, no unwholesome thing; they be the very dainty and pure feeding . . . Here may all manner of persons, men, women, young, old, learned, unlearned, rich, poor, priests, laymen, lords, ladies, officers, tenants, and mean men, virgins, wives, widows, lawyers, merchants, artificers, husbandmen and all manner of persons, of what estate or condition so ever they be, in this book

learn all things what they ought to believe, what they ought to do . . .
Briefly, to the reading of the scripture none can be enemy, but that
either be so sick that they love not to hear of any medicine, or else that
be so ignorant that they know not scripture to be the most healthful
medicine.' It was to be from the Great Bible, with which Cranmer was
so closely associated, that the biblical passages in the Book of Common Prayer [as well as the canticles, the Benedicitie, the Benedictus,
the Magnificat, the Nunc Dimittis] and the Psalter were to be taken.

Although the political scene in Henry VIII's closing years continued very unquiet and for Cranmer personally at times dangerous,
he had turned to experimenting with the use of the vernacular in
worship. He was cautious and even conservative in his approach. In
1541 Henry had ordered that a chapter of the New Testament in
English and after that was completed a chapter from the Old Testament should be read at Matins and Vespers on Sundays and Holy
Days. Next year Cranmer informed Convocation that the king desired
a reformation of the service books, and he may very likely have already
engaged on a draft revision of the breviary.

Two years later Cranmer completed his work on the English litany,
the first fruit of his genius, and a significant landmark in his powers as
translater and composer of English prose. 'Upon the 18 October
[1544]', William Harrison wrote 'the Letany in the english toung is,
by the kinges commahndment, sung openly in Powles in London, and
commaundment geven that it should be sung in the same toung
thorow out all England.' It was by and large a conservative compila-
tion, drawing on the Sarum Litany for Rogation Monday, the eighth
century litany from the Pontifical of Archbishop Egbert of York, a
translation of a medieval litany by Luther, a German litany commissioned by Hermann von Wied, archbishop of Cologne, and a litany
from Marshall's Primer of 1535. But it showed Cranmer's fertile
genius as a translator already at work. Compare, for instance, the
prayer from the Latin of the Sarum rite 'Ab omni malo, libera nos
domine, Ab omni peccato, libera nos domine, abinsidiis diaboli,
libera nos domine and so forth with Cranmer's version 'From all evill
and mischiefe, from sinne, from the crafts and assaults of the divill,
from thy wrath, and from everlasting damnation, Good lord deliver
us.' There is in Cranmer's translation a rising crescendo of language,
sonorous and rhythmical.

C. S. Lewis complained of Cranmer's prose that 'Cranmer always
writes in an official capacity. Everything he says has been threshed out

in a committee.' If this is a valid complaint, and instantly it seems so much more applicable to the Alternative Service Book, it can hardly be applied to the Litany. The Litany was, as F. E. Brightman said, 'not original . . . but had an extraordinary power of absorbing and improving other people's work.' Its language was compelling, imprinted on the mind. 'From all such devils', says Shakespeare in the Taming of the Shrew, 'Good Lord, deliver us', a quotation which shows at once how difficult it is to trace the exact impact of the influence of Cranmer and the Prayer Book for the writing became in some sense an unconscious part of the literary heritage.

In a letter which he wrote to the king on 7 October 1544 Cranmer described his method: 'In which translation, for as much as many of the processions in the Latin [he is referring to the litany] were but barren, as meseemed, and little fruitful, I was constrained to use more than the liberty of a translator: for in some processions I have altered divers words, in some I have added part; in some taken part away; some I have left out whole, either for by cause the matter appeared too little to purpose, or by cause the days be not with us festival days [Egbert's Pontifical, for instance, contained some 96 invocations of the saints] . . . I trust it will much excitate and stir the hearts of all men unto devotion and godliness: but in mine opinion, the song that shall be made there unto would not be full of notes but as near as may be, for every syllable a note, so that it may be sung distinctly and devoutly, as be in the Matins and Evensong, Venite, the Hymns, Te Deum, Benedictus, Magnificat, Nunc Dimittis, and all the Psalms and Versicles.' Characteristically he felt bound to add 'by cause mine English verses lack the grace and facility that I would wish they had, your majesty may cause some other to make them again, that can do the same in more pleasant English and phrase.'

With the death of the monstrous king and the accession of the Protestant boy Edward VI, the new Josiah as Cranmer christened him, a brighter day seemed to dawn. 'Therefore not from the bishop of Rome', so Cranmer addressed the young king at his coronation, 'but as a messenger from my Saviour Jesus Christ, I shall most humbly admonish your royal majesty, what things your highness is to perform. Your majesty is God's vice-regent and Christ's vicar within your own dominions, and to see, with your predecessor Josiah, God truly worshipped, and idolatry destroyed, the tyranny of the bishops of Rome banished from your subjects, and images removed. You are to reward virtue, to revenge sin, to justify the innocent, to relieve the poor, to procure peace, to repress violence and to execute justice throughout your realms.'

Among other matters the ordering of public worship had high priority. It seems that Cranmer had already drawn up drafts, partly based on the revised breviary of Cardinal Quinones, for a revision of the Latin offices.* An Order for Communion, composed in March 1548, provided in the first instance for the insertion of an English litany into the body of the Latin mass, consisting of an exhortation, absolution, comfortable words, prayer before communion, words of administration and blessing, all of which were eventually to find their way into the first Book of Common Prayer.

It is plain that this was already very much in Cranmer's mind, and though the evidence is very tenuous in all probability advanced in draft form. In the early autumn of 1548 a committee was appointed under Cranmer's chairmanship 'to see very shortly', as a royal decree of 23 September 1548 put it, 'one uniform order of worship'. 'A good number of the best learned men reputed within this realm', Cranmer was to write in his defence to Queen Mary in September 1555, 'some favouring the old, some the new learning . . . were gathered together for the reformation of the service of the church, . . . it was agreed by both, without controversy (not one saying the contrary), that the service of the church ought to be in the mother tongue, and that St Paul in the fourteenth chapter to the Corinthians was so to be understanden.' The details of what happened are obscure. The committee which consisted of leading bishops and divines had regular meetings at Windsor Castle and Cranmer's house, Chertsey Abbey, to discuss the drafts. Within three months the work was complete. Although three conservative bishops, Day, Skip and Thirlby opposed the changes, Parliament, at the instigation of the Protector, the Duke of Somerset, passed the Act of Uniformity to which the new prayer book was appended on 21 January 1549. The first copies were immediately on sale, and the prayer book was made obligatory as from the next Whitsunday, 9 June.

It is impossible to be absolutely sure how much of the Prayer Book, whether the translation or the newly composed collects, was Cranmer's own work. As I said earlier the biblical passages were taken from

---

* Two of these survive, one dating from the latter part of Henry's reign was a reform of the breviary, based on Quinones, and the second reducing the hours to two Matins and Evensong.

the Great Bible. But there is everything to make us think that Cranmer had the major responsibility. None of the other members of the committee had either the necessary experience nor the liturgical learning. They may have amended but they can hardly have created. For the past ten years Cranmer had been able to forget the travail of life at court in making drafts, many of which were never to see the light of day. It is surely not going too far to say that Cranmer may well have presented a draft to the committee, for it would have been impossible to have composed the book in little more than three months starting from scratch. Cranmer was the prime mover and the creative spirit in the work, and its prose whether translation or composition bears the distinctive hall-marks of his style.

Even more than the litany the 1549 BCP is a literary and liturgical pastiche. It was culled from a great variety of sources as F. E. Brightman stressed in his masterly work on the English Rite. The breviary of the Franciscan general Quinones, for instance, was the source of the preface which came from Cranmer's first breviary. The Daily offices were a conflation of the monastic hours, Terce, Sext and None were dropped, Matins, Lauds and Prime formed Morning Prayer or Mattins, Vespers and Compline, Evensong. The Epistles and Gospels were from the Great Bible. The collects for the most part came from sixth century sacramentary but Cranmer made a free translation, amending, pruning and paraphrasing. Some he composed himself, the first and second Sundays in Advent, for Christmas Day, Quinquagesima Sunday, Ash Wednesday, the first Sunday in Lent, the first and second Sundays after Easter, and for a number of feast days. The 'Supper of the Lord and the Holy Communion, Commonly Called the Mass' was in many respects conservative, being drawn from the Sarum missal but it had a radical and practical aspect, owing much to Hermann von Wied and the Lutheran church orders. It put forward a new definition of the mass. Cranmer's eucharistic doctrine was a moving spectrum of interpretation. 'I think it convenient', he had written in 1548, 'to use the [English] tongue in the mass, except in certain secret mysteries, where I doubt', but when shortly afterwards he consecrated Ferrar to the see of St Davids English was used throughout. Stephen Gardiner claimed specifically that Cranmer was the author of the 1549 service.

The Communion service was followed by the litany and the occasional services with a catechism which bears the marks of Cranmer's composition inserted between the services of baptism and confirmation. The prayer book ended with an essay entitled 'Of ceremonies, Why some be Abolished and some Retained' and 'certain Notes for the more Plain Explication and Decent Ministration of Things contained in this Book.' The following year an Ordinal was published containing services for the ordination of deacons and priests, and for the consecration of bishops; and John Merbecke provided a musical setting which reflected Cranmer's principal of 'one syllable, one note', embodying the natural speech rhythms of the liturgy.

By any standard the prayer book of 1549 was a major achievement. Cranmer had brought together the five main service books which the medieval clergy had to use, the Missal, the Canon of the Mass, the Breviary, the Book of Divine Offices, the Manual, the occasional services, the Pontifical, containing the ceremonial appertaining to a bishop and the Processional, the musical setting, into a single volume and formed them into a single rite. There had been five uses in the English medieval church, the Sarum use and the uses of York, Hereford, Bangor and Lincoln. Cranmer's conflation of these uses and the redefinition to which he submitted them was an operation of the first magnitude historically and liturgically but perhaps even more they were a triumph of the English language. 'If' as E. C. Ratcliff put it, 'the English liturgy is not incomparable, its language is so.'

It could hardly be expected that the prayer book would be wholly acceptable either to traditionalists or radicals. There was an armed rebellion against its enforcement in the west country which drew from Cranmer a stinging rebuke as well as an apologia for the use of the vernacular. The rebels had complained that the new prayer book was like a Christmas game. 'It is more like a game', Cranmer declared, 'and a fond play to be laughed at of all men, to hear the priest speak aloud to the people in Latin, and none understandeth other. Neither the priest nor his parish wot what they say. And many times the thing that the priest saith in Latin is so fond of itself, that it is more like a play than a godly prayer. But in the English service appointed to be read there is nothing else but the eternal word of God: the new and old Testament is read, that hath power to save your souls.'

Radical Protestant opinion was equally disconcerted by what seemed to its exponents too great an adherence to traditional teaching. In his *Censura* Martin Bucer enunciated some sixty criticisms. Cranmer's own theological views were themselves undergoing some fluctuation, reflecting in part the impressionistic impact of the foreign reformers who were being given favour and patronage at Edward's court, largely at Cranmer's behest. Somerset fell from power and was replaced by the ruthless and disagreeable duke of Northumberland, in religion, if more by expediency than principle, a Protestant hard-liner.

In such circumstances Cranmer took a hand, perhaps the major part, in revising the 1549 Prayer Book. A second Act of Uniformity was passed on 14 April 1552, ordering the new prayer book to come into public use on All Saints Day, 1st November. The revision was in a distinctly Protestant direction; the penitential element at both Matins and Evensong and at the Holy Communion which saw the insertion of the Kyries and the Ten Commandments into the service were emphasised. Much more deliberately designed to refute the tradition-al teaching on the Real Presence and Sacrifice in the Mass, the words of administration showed that the stress was on remembrance rather the manifestation of the real presence in the elements of bread and wine, transformed into Christ's body and blood, and on the indwell-ing faith of the recipient. The collects remained substantially un-changed with one notable exception where Cranmer revised the collect for the festival of St Andrew to rid it of supposed Catholic undertones.* But the book had short life, for the death of Edward VI on 6 July 1553 brought Cranmer's liturgical experiments to an end. In the short Marian reaction he fell a victim to the religious tyranny of the age in which in another role he had been a participant, ironically a victim to that royal supremacy in the church which had been for so long the basic concept to which he had been consistently loyal.

After Mary's death, Elizabeth moved circumspectly. Her own inclinations in religious matters were conservative but for political and personal reasons intrinsically Protestant; yet she wished to satisfy the radicals without alienating the Catholics. In the upshot, by the acts of supremacy and uniformity of 1559, the prayer book of 1552 was revived, shorn of some of its more disagreeable features such as the

---

* 1549. Almighty God which hast given such grace to thy Apostle Saint Andrew, that he counted the sharp and painful death of the cross to be an high honour, and a great glory: Grant us to take and esteem all troubles and adversities which shall come unto us for thy sake as things profitable for us toward the obtaining of everlasting life.

1552. Almighty God who didst give such grace unto thy holy Apostle Saint Andrew, that he readily obeyed the calling of thy son Jesus Christ, and followed him without delay: Grant unto us all, that being called by thy holy word, my forthwith give over ourselves, obediently to follow thy holy commandments.

so-called Black rubric and the vehement condemnation of the pope. By combining the words of administration of both books at the communion the Elizabethan prayer book made possible a latitude of interpretation which was to prove one of the enduring strengths of Anglicanism. In the ensuing years it underwent minor modifications as in 1604 and more substantially in 1662 when it was revised 'for the more proper expressing of some words or phrases of ancient usage in terms more suitable to the language of the present times', though in fact the language had not very significantly changed between 1549 and 1662.* In the main there were to be no significant changes until the semi-abortive measure of 1928 and the Prayer Book Alternative and other Services measure of 1965.

Cranmer had more works to his credit than the prayer book, notably the Homilies, but the prayer book was his great legacy. If it was the product of a corporate mind his was the guiding hand. Some have thought to have detected the hands of Latimer who lodged with Cranmer and in the 1552 book of Hooper but he was the organizer, the adapter and the translator. 'The Book of Common Prayer', W. E. Gladstone wrote to the orthodox prelate, the archbishop of Syra and Tenos, in October 1875, 'supplies the subject-matter of religious worship, and this must vitally enter into the spiritual food of the people, and, in fact, gives them in a very high degree their specific religious tone. 'The Book of Common Prayer', so comments David Daiches, 'remains eloquent testimony to the English genius for preserving continuity amid change.'

What then were the features of Cranmer's prose in so far as it was Cranmer's work which gave it an enduring influence in the history of English literature?

Sixteenth-century English prose was often prolix and long-winded with a particular fondness for alliteration and for using two words where one would do, as much devotional and homiletic writing of the period demonstrates. The English primers with which the Book of Common Prayer bears comparison were of variable value. Two illustrations underline the superiority of the PB's prose style. Compare the phrase in the primer from the Te Deum 'Thee, endeles fadir, every erthe worchipeth'† with the prayer book's 'All the earth do

---

*The principal change was that the Epistles and Gospels were now taken from the authorized version of 1611.

†The original—'Te eternum patrem omnis terra veneratur'.

worship thee, the father everlasting'. Or take another comparison the phrase in the litany which in the primer of 1535 runs 'That thou vouchsaaf to give us fruits of the erthe' and in that of 1539 'That thou vouchsafe to give and preserve the fruits of the earth' with Cranmer's more comprehensive and sonorous 'That it may please thee to give to our use the kindly fruits of the earth as in due time we may enjoy them.' Where the primers translated the original Latin into English, the language of the translation may often appear as unduly sentimental and even gushing. This was something which Cranmer managed to avoid, for his piety is restrained in character and in language; the litany, as one writer has said, became less exclamatory, the baptismal service less dramatic. The liturgical scholar Bishop Frere queried whether Cranmer's translations lost the qualities of terseness and tautness characteristic of the originals. Yet these extended translations gained in rhythym and cadence and appear in general an improvement on the original. The Latin 'peccata' sins becomes 'sins and wickednesses', 'mortifica' 'mortify and kill', videant 'perceive and know', 'tradi' 'to be betrayed and given up'. Eight words of petition in the litany 'ut afflictos et periclitantes respicere et salvare digneris' become 18 in the English translation 'That it may please thee to succour, help and comfort all that be in danger, necessity and tribulation . . .' In fine Cranmer found a free equivalent for the Latin. His translations appear graceful, flexible but normally preserve the meaning of the original. C. L. Feltoe queried whether this was the case. To illustrate his argument he took Cranmer's translation of the Latin collect for the fifth Sunday after Epiphany. The Latin reads 'continua pietate custodi' which Cranmer translated as 'keep continually in the true religion'. Feltoe commented that the word pietas means pity and mercy rather than religion. Yet Stella Brook pointed out that in translating pietas as religion, Cranmer was reverting to an earlier classical meaning of the word, understood as worthiness, dutifulness which could be described comprehensibly as religion. Something which would have been familiar to him (in contemporary humanist scholarship).

Both in his translations and composition Cranmer was most concerned to ensure that what he wrote was faithful to the word of God, and that this should be fully understood by the ordinary man and woman. So he wrote with the intention that what he was writing would have an aural impact. The realization that what he was writing would be heard rather than read explains the importance which in his prose he gave to the accents and stress in the individual sentences. He was in this respect, though it is possible that too much weight has been given to the argument, that he was making a conscious use in English of the *cursus* of medieval Latin, that is the way in which long and short syllables may be arranged or distributed to create a rhythmical prose. 'Rhythmically', I quote C. S. Lewis, 'a sentence may be regarded phonetically like a succession of peaks and valleys, peaks being syllables on which there is a strong accent, creating a strongly supported rhythm.' Examples may be found scattered about his prose: 'Thy bright beams of light', 'born of a pure virgin', 'all desires known'—'our hearts may surely there be fixed where true joys are to be found'—all illustrations of the use of strong syllables. In the last sentence C. S. Lewis found that eight out of sixteen syllables represented peaks. Long monosyllables in one clause may be used to balance short syllables in the next. So we cast away 'the works of darkness' and put upon us the 'armour of light . . .' While Cranmer's conscious use of the *cursus* which he mentioned in his letter to the king should not be overstressed, it certainly helped to create a style that was instinctively balanced and sonorous.

The collects represent Cranmer at his most masterly. They fall into two groups, those which he translated from the Latin which were derived originally from the Gelasian and Gregorian sacramentaries of the sixth century or from the medieval Sarum missal, and those which he composed himself. The latter group includes the final collects at the end of the Communion service, the collects for the first and second Sundays in Advent, for Christmas Day, Quinquagesima, Ash Wednesday, the first Sunday in Lent, the first and second Sundays after Easter and for a number of Saints' days. With a sure touch Cranmer found free equivalents in English for the Latin and if the sense is prescribed by the Latin original they stand on their own as pieces of creative composition. So in the collect for the first Sunday after Epiphany the Latin 'ut et quae agenda sunt videant: et ad implenda que viderint convalescant' is paraphrased as 'that they may both perceive and know what things they ought to do, and also have grace and power faithfully to fulfil the same.' 'In the English form', so Stella Brook comments, 'the compaction of the Latin and the distinctive chime of the inflectional word-play are replaced by the balancing of larger syntactic units.' One has only to compare the collects which Cranmer composed specifically with those which were added in 1662, the collects for the third Sunday in Advent, St

Stephen's Day and some others to see how superior Cranmer was in his capacity to write pure and sonorous prose free from ornateness and prolixity.

Cranmer's instinctive feeling for words appears in his use of word-doubling, 'may . . . perceive and know', 'may have grace and power', one phrase being used to balance another so as to give an integral pattern to the sentence: 'manifold sins and wickedness' as in the General Confession; 'for better, for worse, for richer, for poorer' as in the marriage service 'Cranmer's amazing sensitivity', Stella Brook again, 'to the possibilities of English as a liturgical language produced a homogeneous style that could adapt itself equally to close or free translation or to fresh creation.' Compare the wording in Lady Jane Grey's prayer book 'Holy arte thow, Holy arte thow. Thow arte the Lord God of Hostes' with the prayer book's 'Holy, Holy . . . Lord God of Sabaoth.' Cranmer's prose was clear, straightforward, free from ambiguity, elementally simple, free from euphoristic rhetoric or decorative complexity.

It is perhaps easier to indicate the qualities of Cranmer's prose than to delineate clearly the influence which the Book of Common Prayer to which he was a major contributor and creator had on English literature. In a sense it is immeasurable for the influence of the Book of Common Prayer has to be placed side by side with the translations of the Bible, more especially the Authorized Version. In their impact on English literature the Book of Common Prayer and the Authorized Version were blood brothers.

Certain specific instances underline English writers' indebtedness to Cranmer. In particular John Donne's contemplative poem The Litanie, composed in 1609–10, some five or six years before Donne's ordination to the Anglican ministry, was based to a very striking degree on Cranmer's Litany. Apart from the omission of the concluding supplication, Donne followed the structure of the 1544 Litany very closely, constituting what Helen Gardner considered the 'most Anglican of the Divine Poems'. Less direct in attribution but fundamentally indebted to Cranmerian writing were the poems of George Herbert, more especially his poem A Priest to the Temple, or, The Country Parson His Character and Rule of Holy Life. In his 'character of the Parson', Joseph Sunners wrote, 'Herbert showed himself a devoted son of the Church of England who followed the Prayer Book faithfully if liberally'. 'His obedience and conformitie to the Church and the discipline thereof was singularly remarkable', so reads the preface to the Temple, 'Though he abounded in private devotions, yet went he every morning and evening with his familie to the Church; and by his example, exhortation, and encouragements drew the greater part of his parishioners to accompanie him dayly in the publick celebrations of Divine Service.'

The influence of the Book of Common Prayer is suffused so widely as to become a part of the literary unconscious, of the very weft and texture of English prose. Shakespeare's plays are speckled with allusions to the Book of Common Prayer, the Psalter or the Great Bible. Hamlet refers to 'these pickers and stealers', a reference to the phrase in the Catechism', to keep my hands from picking and stealing': the 'vainpomp and glory of this world' which Cardinal Wolsey was ultimately to deplore recalled the baptismal service. 'We bring our tales to an end,' so Psalm XC v 9 'as it were a tale that is told'. 'Life,' says Macbeth, 'is a tale told by an idiot' 'Life is as tedious as a twice-told tale', so King John. 'I will be brief', says the friar in Romeo and Juliet, 'for my short date of breath is not so long as is a tedious tale'. 'O most gentle pulpiter', Rosalind exclaims in *As You Like It*, 'what tedious homily of love have you wearied your parishioners withal,' and never cried 'Have patience, good people', a reference, if perhaps somewhat uncomplimentary to Cranmer's 34 Homilies.*

Cranmer's prayer book is not unlike Wren's majestic masterpiece St Paul's; if you would seek my memorial, look around you. Kinglake wrote of Lady Hester Stanhope in Eothen, 'She . . . impiously dared, as it was said, to boast some mystic union with the very God of very God', a reference back to the Nicene Creed. In Rose Macaulay's novel, *The Towers of Trebizond*, 'Meg thought it could not be in his nature to attain to true religion and virtue'. 'We talked about gardens and food and the state of Christ's Church militant on earth', Edmund Crispin wrote in the Case of the Gilded Fly. P. D. James's most recent book, *Devices and Desires*, recalls the words of the General Confession 'We have followed too much the devices and desires of our own hearts'.

Take any Dictionary of Quotations and see how many phrases from the Book of Common Prayer have become a part and parcel of the

---

* It has been noted that Falstaff's words to Poins in I Henry IV I ii, 'Well, God give thee the spirit of persuasion and him the ears of profiting, that what thou speakest may move and what he hears may be believed' seems to recall the rhythms and balanced construction of the collects.

common language. From the Prayer Book Psalter (not the authorised version of the Bible): 'like a giant refreshed' (Ps lxxviii, 66), 'the iron entered into his soul', 'olive-branches describing children', 'the pelican in the wilderness', 'flourishing like a green-bay tree', 'by the waters of Babylon'. We can think of spiritual, 'earth to earth', 'ashes to ashes, dust to dust'. The catalogue of verbs, 'read, mark, learn and inwardly digest', recalls the collect for the Second Sunday in Advent. The phrase 'sins of the fathers' recalls the second of the Ten Commandments in the Communion Service: visit the sins of the fathers upon the children unto the third and fourth generation (in the authorised version it reads 'the iniquity of our father').*

To later writers as to some of his contemporaries Thomas Cranmer's career seemed somehow flawed. It was his nature, as the Elizabethan Jesuit Robert Parsons said, 'then and ever after, to run after the time'. He might well seem a fine example of the don who is mistakenly taken from the world of book learning to the world of power politics, becoming involved in games which he could not control and which may even have been outside his comprehension. He had maintained a pretence of loyalty to the pope. He had tolerated the gross appetites of the king, participating in the trials of heretics to the left and right of the religious spectrum. Although he wrote strangely moving letters in defence of Anne Boleyn and Thomas Cromwell, he had not hesitated to accept the royal verdict. After the psychological pressures exercised by the Marian regime he had made a humiliating recantation before he went repentant, dignified and courageous to the stake.

But it is anachronistic to foist the moral judgments of the twentieth century on a sixteenth century churchman. Cranmer has to be seen in the framework of his times. For him the royal supremacy had become the lifeline of his existence. He believed that if he lost Henry's support and he walked a perilous tight rope, then the Protestant reformation in England would itself be imperilled. In the midst of the turmoil of his times, as Peter Brooks has stressed, he presided over a church in transition revising services, reformulating doctrine and re-drafting law, creating a single comprehensive church which was moderate, without papalism, yet in many ways intrinsically catholic. His linguistic artistry was such that he was unquestionably a major contributor to

*Cranmer's genius, not indeed easy to identify, flows like a life-giving blood through the English language. No more tragic step, at least in my view has occurred than the relegation of the BCP to the shelf in favour of the ASB.

the development of the English language. If there are occasional blemishes, if the language is occasionally archaic, yet Cranmer's niche in the history of English literature is assured. 'His merits and services', the Victorian church historian, R. W. Dixon, wrote, 'were greater than his faults. He had gravity, gentleness and innocency: boundless industry and carefulness; considerable power of forecast: and he lived in a high region. He preserved the continuity of the Church of England. He gave to the English Reformation largeness and capacity. In the weakness which he himself admitted he was servile to many influences: he turned himself many ways in the waters, and allowed himself to be carried very far; but this was not altogether to the hurt of posterity. He was a greater man than any of his contemporaries.' Perhaps we can do no better than close with the words which Cranmer himself used in defence of the first Prayer Book, urging that it constituted 'the clear light to our eyes, without the which we cannot see and a lantern unto our feet, without which we would stumble.'

A few days ago I was sent a privately printed book of poems by an old member of my college, David Reid, entitled Brief Interlude which included one which recalled his experience in World War II.

> Migrant through the military years
> In Asia, Africa and Italy,
> Where Cranmer's spirit came to exiled ears,
> Borne on Sunday wings, peregrine and free,
> To manifest the Church whose ritual first
> Put flesh on non-conformist bones.
>
> The voice of martyred Cranmer still rings strong
> Blending with whispered centuries of prayer
> And Tudor-scented dust which lingers long
> Giving me antiquity to share.

A Joint Lecture with the Royal Society and the British Academy

TRANSLATION OR TRANSFORMATION? THE RELATIONS OF LITERATURE AND SCIENCE

GILLIAN BEER

Read 20 April 1989
Rt Hon. Lord Jenkins of Hillhead, FRSL, in the Chair

THE THEME announced for this lecture, 'the presentation of science through literature' might suggest a one-way traffic, as though literature acted as a mediator for a topic (science) that precedes it and that remains intact after its re-presentation. That is not how I understand the relations between the two. I shall emphasize interchange rather than origins and transformation rather than translation. Scientific and literary discourses overlap, but unstably. Victorian writers, scientific and literary, held to the ideal of the 'mother-tongue'; in our own time the variety of professional and personal dialects is emphasised instead. Yet the expectation lingers that it should be possible to translate stably from one to another. This expectation may prove unrealistic.

More is to be gained from analysing the transformations that occur when ideas change creative context and encounter fresh readers. The

★ This is the text of the first lecture on literature and science, sponsored by the Royal Society of Literature, the British Academy and the Royal Society, and given at the Royal Society on 20 April 1989.

fleeting and discontinuous may be as significant in our reading as the secure locking of equivalent meanings. Questions can change their import when posed within different genres. Recognizing scientific reference within works of literature may not be a straightforward a business as it seems. To put it at its most direct: how do we recognize science once it is in literature? Can such reference to scientific material be drained again of its relations within the literary work and returned to autonomy?

Neither literature nor science is an entity and what constitutes literature or science is a matter for agreement in a particular historical period or place. The activities of scientists, and their social and institutional bases, have changed enormously over the past hundred years. More, on the face of it, than those of the writer of literature. But the English language now bears a freight of meaning from very diverse national groups across the world. That is an important change. The present internationalism of both science and literature makes for curious crossplays. I shall examine some examples later in this argument. The movement towards mathematicization has enhanced hopes of a stable community of meaning for scientists at work; the spread of English makes for often delusive accords between different communities of meaning.

In the first part of the lecture I concentrate on some sought-for correspondences between scientific and literary language; in the second part I examine some recent examples of the transformation of scientific materials in literary works. Such analysis reminds us forthwith of the apparent ease with which, in language, we inhabit multiple, often contradictory, epistemologies at the same time, all the time.

AUTHORITATIVE LANGUAGES

In the mid and late nineteenth century the humanities were still in the ascendant in school and university studies, whereas now the appeal to authority is usually in the direction of science. In that way our present situation differs also from that described thirty years ago by C. P. Snow in *The two cultures*.[1]

---

[1]C. P. Snow, *The two cultures and the scientific revolution* (Cambridge: Cambridge University Press, 1959).

The language available alike to nineteenth-century creative writers and scientists had been forged out of past literature, the Bible, philosophy, natural theology, the demotic of the streets or the clubs. Scientists as various as James Clerk Maxwell and Charles Lyell habitually seamed their sentences with literary allusion and incorporated literature into the argumentative structures of their work (as Lyell does Ovid and Clerk Maxwell Tennyson.) The first number of the scientific journal *Nature* (4 November 1869) opened with a set of aphorisms culled from Goethe and selected by Huxley. Huxley describes the journal's aim as 'to mirror the progress of that fashioning by Nature of a picture of herself, in the mind of man, which we call the progress of Science'.[2] 'Progress', 'fashioning', 'picture', 'mirroring', 'Nature herself': the securing of enquiry by means of a stable accord with a sacrilized external world is reinforced by the journal's epigraph from Wordsworth —

> To the solid ground
> Of nature trusts the Mind that builds for aye.

'Ground' in this scientific context condenses the senses 'earth' and 'argument'. That epigraph, with its accompanying image, continues as the bannerhead of the journal, past Maxwell, past Einstein, for almost a hundred years. In 1957 it was shorn of its image but it was retained on each volume title page until 1963, when its anachronism must at last have seemed greater than its annealing powers.

To the Victorians, whether preoccupied with science or literature or politics—and however conscious they might be of the fickleness of signification—the concept of the mother-tongue was crucial. In the case of English the 'mother-tongue' was idealized as the English of past literature above all. Scientific writers in the Victorian period were immersed in the general language of the tribe, yet needed to formulate their own stable professional dialects with which to communicate with each other. By that means they would be able to change the level of description so as to engage with new theoretical and technical questions. They would also limit the range of possible interpretation, and, it was their hope, misinterpretation. But they were reluctant to allow writing on scientific issues to remain on the linguistic periphery. They thus claimed congruity with poetry, perceived as the authoritative utterance within current language.

[2] T. H. Huxley, *Nature* I, (no. I) (1869.

Victorian middle and upper class language was formed by what we might call a parental diad: not only the mother-tongue but the father-tongue shaped the dominant educational ideology. Classical languages played a central role in the education system, a system reserved almost entirely for boys until the late 19th century and taught to them by men. The practice of Victorian scientists of citing classical writing in their work serves several functions: some social, some illustrative, some argumentative. Such allusion effortlessly claimed gender and class community with a selected band of readers; it implied a benign continuity for scientific enquiries with the imaginative past of human society; it could figure the tension between objectivity and affect.

In our own time writers on discourse have emphasised the heterogeneity of dialects within the apparently common tongue, the way in which we never can quite securely translate from one professional or social group to another the intensity, or vacuity, of terms. Terms may be precise and full in one domain, meagre in another, transformed in yet another: 'matter' would be a simple example, or 'select'. Words are also subject to ontological decay: what starts precise and bounded may become neutralized, or soggy. When George Eliot's novel *Daniel Deronda* first appeared, both R. H. Hutton and George Saintsbury objected in their reviews to the description of the heroine's 'dynamic glance' as being pedantic and over-scientific.[3] Hardly the objection that such a clichéd phrase would raise now.

Words are impressed with the shared assumptions, with the things *not said* of each group, just as much as they are with their shared assertions. But none of us is a member of one social and linguistic group only. We live, therefore, in a variety of conflicted epistemologies. Scientific workers strive to contain their procedures within a single epistemological frame, but cannot exempt them from further and other construals. We experience every day, and we condense that experience in speaking and listening, as co-workers, shoppers, friends, researchers, women or men, perhaps parents, lovers, certainly political activists or quietists, members willy-nilly of local, national and global communities at a particular moment in historical time. Some terms transfer across all these zones, particularly those terms that have to do with kinship, commerce, measurement, conflict. They shift scale and energy as they go.

[3] Collected in D. Carroll (ed.), *George Eliot the critical heritage* (London: Routledge, 1971), pp. 369, 374.

Much literature of the late twentieth century is proudly parodic, presenting puns as the profoundest rather than the lowest form of wit. The preference for improbable simultaneities that hold unlike together goes alongside the emphasis in wave-particle theory on unreconciled complementarity. As Edwin Morgan puts it in the briefest of his six particle poems:

> The particle that decided
> got off its mark, but died.[4]

The word 'decided' by the act of decision withers to its four last letters i d e d and 'died'. How to explain such proximities?

Gerald Holton speaks of the 'themata' of a period, a term which is an attempt to move away from the concept *Zeitgeist* with its inherent animism.[5] The banishing of *Zeitgeist* has usefully uncovered a series of difficulties: how to describe the relations between intellectual fields within a historical period? How to relate them to social and economic movements? How to articulate the interactions between apparently remote preoccupations? How to analyse the close written relations between authors who probably never read each others' work? How to explain the concurrent appearance of similar ideas in science and in literature without inevitably forging causal links? And how to avoid stabilizing the argument so that one form of knowledge becomes again the origin of all others?

Major changes have taken place since the time of the controversy over the 'two cultures'. Scientific events are now the daily currency of our newspapers. A great writer, Primo Levi, has, in *The Periodic Table* and other works, demonstrated that being human and being a scientist may be the same heroic task when the worst comes.[6] A number of working scientists, as well as many philosophers, have analysed the potency of language in their own practice. Writers as various as François Jacob and Michel Serres have emphasised the simultaneity of science and myth as systems for containing (and constraining) possibility. Some scientists have expressed scientific controversy and theory in non-mathematical terms accessible to general intelligent readers: one thinks, among others, of Stephen Jay

---

[4] E. Morgan, *Poems of thirty years* (Manchester: Carcanet Press, 1982), p. 388.
[5] G. Holton, *The thematic origins of scientific thought: Kepler to Einstein* (Cambridge, Mass: Harvard University Press, 1973).
[6] P. Levi, *The periodic table* (London: Michael Joseph, 1985).

Gould, Stephen Weinberg, Steven Rose, Stephen Hawking, Ilya Prirogine, Richard Dawkins.

Such writing joins a powerful tradition of re-imagined science, represented among the Victorians by writers such as John Tyndall, T. H. Huxley, James Clerk Maxwell, Richard Proctor, W. K. Clifford. In our own century no-one has surpassed the condensed lucidity of Eddington who, for the time of reading, allows the reader to comprehend scientific problems well beyond his or her intellectual reach, though it has to be acknowledged that the burst of clarity is not secure for ever. Alongside him in the late twenties and thirties were figures such as James Jeans and Julian Huxley and H. G. Wells, who elucidated scientific questions in such a way that readers were aware not of the remoteness but of the urgent closeness of those questions to the practical, emotional, political, and economic issues particular to the times. They were made aware, too, of endlessly recurring issues in human society and in life beyond the human.

C. P. Snow's claim that 'the intellectual life of the whole of western society is increasingly being split into two polar groups' excluded further intellectual and cultural groups from consideration.[8] Intellectual life does not take place only among literary intellectuals and physical scientists though those milieus happened to be the ones that Snow knew best. His neglect of other intellectual and artistic concerns falsified the map from the outset. Now, since the expansion of higher education in Britain in the 1960s, his complaints (salient perhaps at the time and, indeed, helping towards the expansion) seem to treat remotely of a dwindling class of literateurs, *not* our main problem now. (Though it is striking to see Peter Ackroyd's new novel *First light* being taken to task by reviewers for poeticizing the Uncertainty Principle.)[9]

Another, more general though shifty, source of understanding has become available. The power of television to represent scientific thinking in the form *simultaneously* of words and images has opened

[7] F. Jacob, *The possible and the actual* (New York: Random House, 1982), p. 9: 'myths and science fulfil a similar function: they both provide human beings with a representation of the world and of the forces that are supposed to govern it. They both fix the limits of what is considered as possible.' M. Serres, *Hermes: literature, science, philosophy* (Baltimore and London: Johns Hopkins Press, 1983), especially 'The Origin of Language: biology, information theory, and thermodynamics', pp. 71–83.
[8] C. P. Snow, op. cit. p. 3.
[9] P. Ackroyd, *First Light* (London: Hamish Hamilton, 1989, p. 3.

access to issues hard properly to represent in words alone. I am sure that working scientists flinch at some of the simplifications and misprisions that result, since at some point algebra must begin, but the spirited leap of enquiry generated both by the works of high popularization and by translation for the screen means that scientific work at present enters the concourse of interpretation rapidly and powerfully. It becomes part of the imaginative currency of the community. It is set in multiple interpretative relationships and helps to construe the times. All the more, science has itself to become more conscious of how it depends on language and on society.

Indeed, the new alliances between scientists and humanists in a bleak economic and educational environment in this country for higher education should not make us too sanguine; they may themselves be a symptom of the extent of the danger we face, which obliges the sinking of real differences.

In preparing this lecture I was ruefully aware of that concourse of dialects—that diversity of assumptions and foreknowledge—active in such a group as we are today. I am not a scientist: my concern is language, representation, and reception. Our special skills do not fall in line with each other. But we do not need to disguise or discard these incongruities. No 'ingenuous transposition' (in Umberto Eco's words) is possible from one genre to another.[10] But neither should transformations be seen as errors or wastage. Snow wrote scornfully of poets 'Now and then one used to find poets conscientiously using scientific expressions, and getting them wrong—there was a time when 'refraction' kept cropping up in verse in a mystifying fashion'.[11] Perhaps the key word there is 'conscientiously', but it seems unlikely that Snow would have liked such fleeting allusions any better had he acknowledged their hedonism. He was hoping, it seems, for perfect gridding.

The reception of ideas outside the immediate circle of co-workers hardly ever is systematic. Many simultaneous kinds of description are necessary; such descriptions do not all converge; understanding works as often recursively as progressively. In scientific writing as in other creative writing we are reading forms of description; to quote Umberto Eco again: 'Indeterminacy, complementarity, noncausality

[10] U. Eco, *The role of the reader* (Bloomington, Ind., 1979), p. 66.
[11] Snow, op. cit., p. 16.

are not *modes of being* in the physical world, but *systems for describing it* in a convenient way'.[12]

Faraday made this same point about how the authority of language misleads once terms are received as 'physical truths'. In a letter to Maxwell on the problematical significance of the term *force* he remarks 'experimentalists on force generally . . . receive that description of gravity as a physical truth, and believe that it expresses all, and no more than all, that concerns the nature and locality of the power. To these it limits the formation of their ideas, and the direction of their exertions' (23 November 1857). Faraday continues, despite his aware-ness of the cramping effects of terminology, by asking Clerk Maxwell whether it may not be possible for mathematicians to express their 'conclusions . . . in common language as fully, clearly, and definitely as in mathematical formulae? . . . translating them out of their hieroglyphics, that we also might work upon them by experiment'.[13]

SEEKING A COMMON TONGUE

A recurrent game of courtesy and reassurance played between scien-tists and other creative thinkers and writers is that of equalizing their concerns, seeing the diversity of their projects as yet part of a common pursuit. So Schrödinger in the 1930s takes up the concept 'homo ludens' and speaks of the essential human 'surplus' that is play, seeing it expressed in card games, literature, conversation, the making of scientific theory.[14] So Helmholtz in the 1870s, having warned against the use of empty big words and the easy manufacture of hypotheses, asserted:

[12] Eco, op. cit. For a discussion of the functions of description see G. Beer 'problems of description in the language of discovery' in G. Levine (ed.) *One culture: essays in science and literature* (Madison, Wisconsin: University of Wisconsin Press, 1987) pp. 35–38.
[13] L. Campbell & W. Garnett, *The life of James Clerk Maxwell* (London: Macmillan, 1882), p. 289–290.
[14] E. Schrödinger, *Science and the human temperament* (London: Allen and Unwin, 1935), p. 23. See E. M. MacKinnon, *Scientific explanation and atomic physics* (Chicago and London: University of Chicago Press, 1982) for helpful discussion of the views on language of Bohr, Heisenberg, Schrödinger and Einstein. See also B. R. Wheaton, *The tiger and the shark: empirical roots of wave-particle dualism* (Cambridge: Cambridge University Press, 1983) for an excellent account of the epistemological debates among physicists in the 1920s and 30s.

The first discovery of a new law, is the discovery of a similarity which has hitherto been concealed in the course of natural processes. It is a manifestation of that which our forefathers in a serious sense described as 'wit', it is of the same quality as the highest performances of artistic perception in the discovery of new types of expression.[15]

The emphasis in Helmholtz's remark is on simultaneity and diversity as together forming fresh concepts, just as wit in poetry condenses absolutely for the moment what has seemed separate, and that in language may separate again. Eighty odd years later than Helmholtz, Heisenberg, drawing on his discussions with Bohr, turns not to the compression of wit but to the expansiveness of natural language (that is conversational speech) as his point of comparison with the discursive practices of science:

one of the most important features of the development and analysis of modern physics is the experience that the concepts of natural language, vaguely defined as they are, seem to be more stable in the expansion of knowledge than the precise terms of scientific language, derived as an idealization from only limited groups of phenomena.[16]

The 'vagueness' in natural language in Heisenberg's terms is a result of multivocality, the way in which a single word may cover a broad range of significations. From among these, the most needed meaning of the moment will be sharply held in focus while the rest remain in shadow. The shadowing, but not evanishing, of counter-significations is a sought effect in much literature, an effect that often dramatizes the re-emergence of repressed senses.

For communication among scientific workers, however, a necessary condition for professional interchange is usually held to be a stable locking of single signification. That is one reason why Peter Medawar in his tonic lecture of 1968 on science and literature flouted the courtesies between the two domains and curtailed the high-minded modesty of expressions such as those I have just quoted: 'The case I shall find evidence for is that when literature arrives, it expels

[15] H. Helmholtz, 'On thought in medicine', in his *Popular lectures on scientific subjects* (second series) (London: Longmans, Green and Co., 1884), p. 227.
[16] W. Heisenberg, *Physics and philosophy: the revolution in modern science* (New York: Harper and Row, 1958), p. 200.

science'.[17] The nub of his argument was his mistaken association of 'rhetoric' only with 'obscurity'.

It is always, let us note, easier to descry rhetoric in retrospect and to analyse the persuasive elements in theories no longer current. But the hope that, within language, words or syntax can be detained within the order of single meaning relies upon a tight contraction of readership, rather than on the terms employed. Bertrand Russell's tart account in *The scientific outlook* of the linguistic problems of physics touches on the helpless largesse of language: 'Ordinary language is totally unsuited for expressing what physics really asserts, since the words of everyday life are not sufficiently abstract. Only mathematics and mathematical logic can say as little as the physicist means to say'.[18]

When Bruno Latour and Steve Woolgar studied the life of a lab for a year as anthropologists, their first strong observation was that they were watching a tribe addicted to inscription. They write:

> After several further excursions into the bench space, it strikes our observer that its members are compulsive and almost manic writers . . . This appears strange because our observer has only witnessed such diffidence in memory in the work of a few particularly scrupulous novelists . . . Our anthropologist is thus confronted with a strange tribe who spend the greatest part of their day coding, marking, altering, correcting, reading, and writing.[19]

Unsurprisingly, the workers in the lab vehemently resisted this description of their activities. Their writing was *about* something, something out there, they argued, and inscription was simply an agency, not in itself an end.

The implicit contrary was with imaginative writing that draws on no stable ulterior world and makes of the activity of writing a topic as well as a medium. Leaving aside for now the improbable assumption that the composition in science of a world 'out there' eschews rhetoric, we may yet assent to a difference between the linguistic position of creative writer and scientist. For one thing, the scientist is involved with many more semiological and gestural systems in the work-place

---

[17] P. Medawar, 'Science and literature', in his *Pluto's kingdom* (Oxford: Oxford University Press, 1982), p. 43.
[18] B. Russell, *The scientific outlook* (London: Allen and Unwin, 1931), p. 85.
[19] B. Latour & S. Woolgar, *Laboratory life: the construction of scientific facts*, 2nd edn. (Princeton: Princeton University Press, 1986) esp. pp. 45–53.

than is the writer: in particular, apparatus, the time-span of an experiment, co-workers in conversation, observers. Creative writing emphazises writing process and calls attention to the reader's activities as reader. The scientific paper, with its tightly ritualized succession of sections, its invariant procedures of description, claims an authoritative retrospect towards the knowledge it produces. Closure has already been completed, as the expression 'writing up' as opposed to writing, claims. The process of experiment, research, thinking, however, is continuing alongside, and there is a sense in which the scientific paper is simply a shedding from that more fundamental and complex activity. For that reason, the notion bruited in justification of Government cutbacks that it is possible to tap into others' research by means of the scientific literature alone in quite misguided.

One of the primary functions of technical language is to keep non-professionals out. There are good reasons for this desire. The closed readership enables precise conceptual exchange and continuance. The sustained achievement of agreed meaning may, however, be at the cost of effective secrecy, even, at worst, of mandarin enclosure. That is one reason (though there are others) why the laboratory has been so often represented in Gothic mode as a secret place where arcane events take place (as in Mary Shelley's *Franken-stein*), where personality is voided (as in Nigel Dennis's *Cards of identity*), or even where the bounds of the human are undermined in a Sadeian promiscuity of hybridization (as in H. G. Wells's *The island of Dr Moreau*). In much science fiction the laboratory becomes a dystopic site where experiments release threatening forms of the future. This Faustian, or occult, characterization is associated with the exclusion of outsiders and the difficulty of interpreting the unfamiliar semiological systems of the lab. Latour and Woolgar offer themselves as comic versions of the naive observer unable to interpret along the grain of the community's assumptions and therefore able to descry activities of which the tribe is unaware, refusing to interpret those activities in terms acceptable to the tribe's internal systems. Very recently, in her collection of poems *Electroplating the baby*, Jo Shapcott has alluded to and subverted Latour and Woolgar further in her poem 'Love in the lab'. The lovers undermine classification by removing the last vestiges of language, tearing the labels off all the jars.[20]

[20] J. Shapcott, *Electroplating the baby* (Newcastle-upon-Tyne: Bloodaxe Books, 1988), pp. 42–3.

Literature cannot, even if it would, take on the task of technical translator when scientists find themselves from time to time in the dilemma that their scrupulousness has sustained agreed meaning but rendered their knowledge and purpose inscrutable to others beyond the trained circle.

Fortunately, however, language, even technical language, is potentially transgressive. As soon as terms get outside the interactive eyes of co-workers, unregarded senses loom up. In *Darwin's plots* I demonstrated the effects of this phenomenon by analysing some of the contradictory significances that Darwin's writing acquired in broader Victorian culture. So, for example, Darwin reserves the word 'race' in a discussion in *The origin of species* to the cultivation of cabbages, but cannot corral it long in that garden-plot.[21]

Sometimes scientists have chosen to draw common terms into technical functions and so to assert a continuity with ordinary experience while designating a specific new signification. We see that phenomenon in the current fashion for belle-lettristic terms such as 'quark', 'charm' and 'black hole'. Such terms allow ontological leeway while theory is being formed; the novelty of the terms does not prematurely foreclose theoretical possibilities, as a more rigorously positivist terminology would do. Such transposed terms also significantly open up highly technical usages to the creative reception—and sometimes misprision—of non-scientists who may thus pursue implications not bounded by the initiating theorems.

Questions of nomenclature in the later 19th century became connected with current movements in language theory and nationalist practice. For example, P. G. Tait, reviewing W. K. Clifford's *Elements of dynamic part I: Kinematic* in *Nature* in 1878, is disturbed by the variety of 'new and very strange nomenclature' and records his dismay at 'an apparently endless array of such new-fangled terms as Pedals, Rotors, Cylindroids, Centrodes, Kites, Whirls, and Squirts! . . . Something, it seems, *must* be hard in a text-book —simplify the Mathematic, and the Anglic (i.e. the English) immediately becomes perplexing'.[22]

Clifford was, in fact, much influenced in his linguistic practice by the work of the philologist, poet and folklorist William Barnes and by

---

[21] G. Beer, *Darwin's plots: evolutionary narrative in Darwin, George Eliot, and nineteenth century fiction* (London: Routledge, 1983).

[22] P. G. Tait, review of *Elements of dynamic part I: kinematic* by W. K. Clifford, in *Nature*, (1878), p. 91.

Barnes's attempt to winnow the foreign elements from English and retrieve a folk-tongue, conceived as forthright, egalitarian, poetic, and truth-telling. Here, scientific discourse claims authority from a revivified common tongue. Very recently, Benoit Mandelbrot (1982) announces that for his fractal geometry he has invented a set of domesticated Gothic terms that combine the grotesque and the humdrum in ways that reassure and yet break bounds. He coins words from what he calls 'the rarely borrowed vocabularies of the shop, the home, and the farm. Homely names make the monster easier to tame. For example, I give technical meaning to *dust*, *curd*, and *whey*'.[23] Elsewhere in the essay he offers 'Cross Lumped Curdling Monsters' and 'Knotted Peano Monsters, Tamed.'

A verbal mimesis of his own theoretical work is implied, in which the random, the inordinate, the non-Euclidian is granted an appropriate language that bulges, miniaturizes and grows gargantuan, constantly shifting across registers of scale and distance to achieve its imaginative effects. He domesticates and enchants his terms. By these means a non-mathematical reader can glimpse the implications of the theorems that are interspersed between the sentences.

LOCAL AND TOTAL REFERENCE

One of the problems in critical exposition and analysis is the desire to offer an account that will penetrate the entire system of a work and riddle its completeness. A kind of professionalism seems to be implied by such an enterprise, and, of course, sometimes it is. But there is a need, if we are to appraise the presences of scientific ideas and activities in literature, to take account also of the local: the fugitive allusion, the half-understood concept, the evasive reference whose significance takes us only some way. I shall show material of that kind gathering power from its fleetingness in *White noise*, one of the most reviewed of recent novels.[24] But equally, fundamental narrative hopes and fears may be renewed and re-shaped by the implications of current scientific theories: for the nineteenth-century reader, descent and variation; for ourselves, information-theory and entropy.

[23] B. Mandelbrot, *The fractal geometry of nature* (San Francisco: W. H. Freeman and Co., 1982) pp. 5, 125. For an analysis of chaos theory in relation to literature see Katherine Hayles's forthcoming study *Chaos. bound.*
[24] D. DeLillo, *White noise* (London: Pan Books, 1986).

How shall we discern such shifts of signification at work? These re-interpretations of significant story may be expressed in the ordering of the narrative rather than declaring themselves in the language of the text; they may be figured in disarrangements, for example, of what Propp took to be the necessary and universal syntax of storytelling.[25] Pynchon's *The crying of lot 49* might serve as an example there.[26] Or, the implications of scientific enquiry may be pursued obsessionally so as to stretch the reader's experience beyond the ordinary registers of sense-experience. Stanislaw Lem's *Fiasco* is a powerful instance of this capacity.[27]

It turns out not always to be a simple matter to re-distil ideas absorbed into other formations. The implications of scientific ideas may manifest themselves in narrative organizations. They may be borne in the fleeting reference more often than in the expository statement, condensed as metaphors or skeined out as story, alive as joke in the discordances between diverse discursive registers. Lightness and suspicion may tell more than scrutiny and exposition.

Scientific material does not have clear boundaries once it has entered literature. Once scientific arguments and ideas are read outside the genre of the scientific paper and the institution of the scientific journal, change has already begun. Genres establish their own conditions which alter the significance of ideas expressed within them. When concepts enter different genres they do not remain intact. Readerships, moreover, are composed not only of individuals but of individuals reading within a genre. So, for example, those whose profession happens to be science do not read novels or poems simply *as scientists* but as readers newly formed by the possibilities of the genre within which their reading is engaged. The readerships implied by the forms and language of novels and poems are more various than those implied by scientific papers.

Yet, although each genre establishes expectations, these expectations cannot be enforced. No genre can preclude the reader's invocation of other knowledge, other questions, than those manifestly indicated by the text. Such other knowledge, other questions, lie latent in the work's terms and forms, waiting for the apt and inappropriate reader. There is therefore always the possibility of a

---

[25] V. Propp, *Morphology of the folktale* (2nd edn) (Austin, Texas: University of Texas, Press, 1968).
[26] T. Pynchon, *The crying of lot 49* (Harmondsworth: Penguin, 1967).
[27] S. Lem, *Fiasco* (London: Andre Deutsch, 1987).

vacillation of meaning, a chording of significance, that will break through generic constraints, whether the genre be that of poem, drama, novel, scientific paper.

Lem, moreover, touches on a paradox always at play in narrative, even at its most unruly: its tendency to align itself with a purposive explanation of the world it describes. Narrative and propositional prose alike have difficulty in paying attention to the non-purposive:

> here nothing served a purpose—not ever, not to anyone—and that here no guillotine of evolution was in play, amputating from every genotype whatever did not contribute to survival, nature, constrained neither by the life she bore nor by the death she inflicted, could achieve liberation, displaying a prodigality characteristic of herself, a limitless wastefulness, a brute magnificence that was useless, an eternal power of creation without a goal, without a need, without a meaning.[28]

Not only single lexical items but whole arguments may have residual and unused resources available to those outside the first circle of reception and debate. Left-over questions implicit in scientific theories may pose themselves anew, or for the first time, in terms that draw upon further—sometimes quite other—resources within a historical moment. The left-over or unraised questions that later surface have most often to do with social order, survival, authority and the quarrel between providence and chance. That is to say, the questions are not themselves framed in terms that will yield once and for all to confirmation or disconfirmation. The questions provoked by scientific writing are recurrent questions that outgo current answers but adopt the terms of current theory.

So, in a recent highly-praised novel, *White noise*, Don DeLillo's serious comedy about fear of death finds its terms in 'waves and radiation' (as the first book is entitled), in the release of noxious gases, the change in weather patterns and in the bricolage of information flowing in through many technological channels. It stills from time to time upon the question of the married pair:

> Who will die first?
> This question comes up from time to time, like where are the car keys. It ends a sentence, prolongs a glance between us. I wonder if

---

[28] Lem, p. 30.

the thought itself is part of the nature of physical love, a reverse Darwinism that awards sadness and fear to the survivor. Or is it some inert element in the air we breathe, a rare thing like neon, with a melting point, an atomic weight?[29]

The novel's characters find comfort in the homely high-tech profusion of the supermarket where peripatetic consumers discover taxonomic order and global plenitude upon the shelves (the supermarket is, I would suggest, the modern Great Exhibition). There, social encounters with acquaintances are brief, benign, spontaneous and non-committal. The ephemeral sumptuousness of the supermarket staves off closure. Because its description invokes lists, it promises endlessness. All the more does dread of death lurk in its aisles, DeLillo suggests.

What, we may ask, does science contribute to this work? The novel certainly includes no expository account of scientific developments, nor more than allusive gestures towards wave-particle conundrums and information theory. But the writing depicts a society whose determining circumstances are the direct outcome of applied science: the train loaded with toxic chemicals, the excellent swift flight of foodstuffs to the supermarket shelves, their gleaming preservation, the radio, the television and telerecorder, the telephone—all those insistent and contingent carriers of messages, few of which are designed for any one recipient, many indeed eerily self-contained in their endless outflow of information. The 'incessant bombardment of information' needs the occasional catastrophe to break it up. 'We're suffering from brain fade' argues one character: 'The flow is constant . . . Words, pictures, numbers, facts, graphics, statistics, specks, waves, particles, motes. Only a catastrophe gets our attention.'[30]

Surface and depth have become indistinguishable; the old spatial hierarchies inconsequential. The irresoluteness of the novel's narrative voice eschews explanation: the family man who speaks the tale is head of Hitler Studies at the College on the Hill and evidences no sense of difficulty about the bland lack of connection between his academic studies and his life. The society imaged is, moreover, one whose deepest disquiets are the outward ripples of fundamental scientific theory, particularly the insistence in entropy on increasing disorganization, and the simultaneous life and death of space-time

[29] DeLillo, op. cit., p. 15.
[30] DeLillo, op. cit., p. 66.

phenomenology. The novel refuses decisive futures, closures, is punctuated by the barren poetry of overheard utterances from radio and television shorn of context. *Déja vu* is the first clinical symptom experienced by victims of the chemical catastrophe that takes place in Delillo's novel. The reference in this novel to *déja vu* is *both* to nature of parody and to the temporal-causal problems raised by the work of Bohr, Heisenberg, and Schrödinger.[31]

Schrödinger's cat is a frequent presence in modern literature, giving the title to Robert Anton Wilson's cult trilogy of the early 1980s[32] and working as fable in a piece such as this by the distinguished Australian poet, Gwen Harwood.[33]

Schödinger's Cat Preaches to the Mice

Silk-whispering of knife on stone,
due sacrifice, and my meat came.
Caressing whispers, then my own
choice among laps by leaping flame.

What shape is space? Space will put on
the shape of any cat. Know this:
my servant Schrödinger is gone
before me to prepare a place.

So worship me, the Chosen One
in the great thought-experiment.
As in a grave I will lie down
and wait for the Divine Event.

---

[31] A. Eddington, *New pathways in science* (Cambridge: Cambridge University Press, 1935): 'As a conscious being I am involved in a story. The perceiving part of my mind tells me a story of the world about me. . . . As a scientist I have become mistrustful of this story. In many instances it has become clear that things are not what they seem to be. According to the story teller I have now in front of me a substantial desk; but I have learned from physics that the desk is not at all the continuous substance that it is supposed to be in the story'. (p. 1) Compare also B. Russell, *The ABC of relativity* (London: Kegan Paul, 1926), p. 226: 'What we know of the physical world . . . is much more abstract than was formerly supposed . . . Of the bodies themselves . . . we know so little that we cannot even be sure that they are anything: they *may* be merely groups of events in other places, those events which we should naturally regard as their effects.'
[32] R. A. Wilson, *Schrödinger's cat*, I. *The universe next door* (London: Sphere, 1980); II. *The trick top hat* (1981); III, *The homing pigeons* (1982).
[33] G. Harwood, *Bone scan* (London: Agnus and Robertson, 1988), pp. 26–7.

The lid will close. I will retire
from sight, curl up and say Amen
to geiger counter, amplifier,
and a cylinder of HCN.

When will the geiger counter feel
decay, its pulse be amplified
to a current that removes the seal
from the cylinder of cyanide?

Dead or alive? The case defies
all questions. Let the lid be locked.
Truth, from your little beady eyes,
is hidden. I will not be mocked.

Quantum mechanics has no place
for what's there without observation.
Classical physics cannot trace
spontaneous disintegration.

If the box holds a living cat
no scientist on earth can tell.
But I'll be waiting, sleek and fat.
Verily, all will not be well.

if, to the peril of your souls,
you think me gone. Know that this house
is mine, that kittens by mouse-holes
wait, who have never seen a mouse.

(From *Bone Scan* by G. Harwood, published by Angus and
   Robertson, reproduced by kind permission of the publishers.)

Is the cat alive or dead? Observing falsifies the answer, Schrödinger
suggests. Harwood here wittily provides a false solution from another
scientific domain: the cat is never safely dead because kittens are born
with the same genetic information, watching by mouse-holes before
they have encountered a mouse. And is God ever safely dead? The
invocation at once of Biblical language and of Schrödinger's thought-
experiment condenses sardonically the menace of returning authority, of descent and instinct as recurrent power, of time disturbed.

This double dread, of order and disorder, is a powerful cultural
story—perhaps the most powerful in the period of post-modernism
since it emphasizes at once the random and the energy of secret

plotting. Like another major American novel, Thomas Pynchon's *The Crying of lot 49*, with its invocation of Maxwell's Demon both as part of the plot and an image for plotting. DeLillo (and in some measure Harwood) turn the reader's attention upon the intrinsication of scientific and literary intelligence, intelligence in both senses, as percipience and spying.

INTERCONNECTION AND INTERNATIONALISM

The alarm in much recent writing is less about the separation of two cultures than about their volatile implication. That may be more typical of American literature than of writing in England. It certainly has something to do with the knowledgeability of a society where many universities routinely run courses generically known as 'Physics for Poets' and scientists must take courses in literature. But although education systems differ, the internationalism of literature in English, like the internationalism of science, is now compelling. This has produced thematics of its own.

The internationalism of both science and literature sets up new tensions between the local and the total. The dreads of particular nations within supra-national culture are focused in the figure of the spy; even more, of the double-agent whose loyalties can never be pinned down. Scientists and writers have allegiances within and beyond national boundaries. Moreover, contradictory ideals are composed within the international community of science: both the rapid free movement of information within the professional community and the competitive secrecy of teams seeking to outdo others. In creative writing in English a different but now wholly unrelated phenomenon can be observed. That phenomenon is the now supra-national availability of English as a lingua franca, and also as a literary language with very diverse ideological and creative meaning for writers in particular countries: in India, in the United States, in the Philippines, in Nigeria, in the Caribbean, in Scotland, for example. It is no longer possible even to pretend that English belongs exclusively to the English and it is necessary now to speak of literature in English as much as English literature. The spy story, with its accoutrements of high-tech information, its trafficking in secret fundamental scientific research, is a new myth generated by the national against supra-national struggle. Frequently its function is to give satisfying vent to a base nationalism that finds itself forbidden expression in polite ideological society.

Tom Stoppard's recent play *Hapgood* includes that level of meaning, though it has other more sophisticated tasks.[34] Stoppard uses the vocabulary and ideas of quantum mechanics to organize his drama —or is the drama an allegorized lecture in quantum mechanics? The play is peculiarly tender towards some forms of English society such as prep school boys playing football. The drama zealously works out the image of the spy, of intelligence and observation, of polyglot communities and the secret command of other tongues, the superposing of contradictory possibilities. The title, Hapgood, proffers reversed indications: 'Good Hap', lucky chance; and uses the designed lucky chance that the word *happens* to sound like (but is not quite identical with) the name of the scientist-theologian Habgood, Archbishop of York. The compactedness of the title is an indication of the close-wrought, yet skittish, quality of the play. There is no reason to expect a solemn or respectful treatment of scientific ideas in literary works.

Stoppard's theatrical pyrotechnics are as closely controlled, and as vacillating, as any proper realization of Heisenberg's uncertainty principle could aim to be:

> Kerner: The particle world is the dream world of the intelligence officer. An electron can be here or there at the same moment. You can choose; it can go from here to there without going in between; it can pass through two doors at the same time, or from one door to another by a path which is there for all to see until someone looks, and then the act of looking has made it take a different path. Its movements cannot be anticipated because it has no reasons. It defeats surveillance because when you know what it's doing you can't be certain where it is, and when you know where it is you can't be certain what it's doing: Heisenberg's uncertainty principle; and this is not because you're not looking carefully enough, it is because there is *no such thing* as an electron with a definite position and a definite momentum; you fix one, you lose the other, and it's all done without tricks, it's the real world, it is awake.

> Hapgood: Joseph, please explain to me about the twins.
> Kerner: I just did but you missed it.[35]

---

[34] T. Stoppard, *Hapgood* (London: Faber, 1988). Stoppard prefaces the play with an epigraph from Richard Feynman's *The character of physical law*.
[35] Stoppard, op. cit., p. 48.

The dramatic problem Stoppard encounters is that the speed of exposition and enactment leaves the audience, like many of the characters, bemused. And the solution (which has to do with multiple sets of twins) baffles the viewer in a way that rebuffs the apparent contract of the 'detective story' to provide a solution permitting a stable tracking back to explanatory origins.

Of course, that is also the point of the play. It enacts the salient difficulties of the theory to which it refers. A familiar trope of stage-craft and of fiction (the twins, the doubles, familiar to us from Shakespearean comedy on) here produces an ironic strain not only between verbal practices but between the possible styles of enactment within scientific theory and in drama. For if the drive in the discourse of quantum physics has been to obliterate the picture and the model, images are inevitably re-introduced by the physical presence of bodies on a stage. The shift of genre produces a transformation that jars with the attempt verbally to translate the concepts of physics.

How then do we recognize the activities of science in literary works if translation will not suffice and transformation may invert the initiating meaning? Fugitive reference need not imply slight meaning. To discover the effects of scientific activity in literary works we need to look not for explanatory or systematic discussion but rather for ironic doubling of reference or the disturbing of authoritative story.

The anthropologist Clifford Geertz in 'Common Sense as a cultural system' sets different authoritative stories on a level with each other, and with what he sees as the improvident claims of common sense to universality: 'Like *Lear*, the New Testament, or quantum mechanics, common sense consists in an account of things which claims to strike at their heart'.[36] Lyotard has argued that our age is characterized by the break up of grand narratives, the loss of authority for scientific knowledge and language alike. His claim is, naturally, the grandest narrative of all: the über-narrative that reflects on götterdämmerung. He claims the end-position, from which summary and fade alike can be conjured.[37] But authoritative narratives have a way of re-forming. Fundamental assumptions may leave slight traces on the surface of writing. Sometimes assumptions declare themselves instead in the order of narrative or in the juxtaposition of diverse sorts of language.

[36] C. Geertz, *Local knowledge: further essays in interpretive anthropology* (New York: Basic Books, 1983), p. 84.
[37] J-F. Lyotard, *The post modern condition: A report on knowledge* (Manchester: Manchester University Press, 1984).

New orderings of knowledge will be sprung with the tensions of form as well as of description, abutting, sometimes merging with, but always casting light upon prior constructions of meaning, their decay, their tenacity.

Science is not a single origin, with literature, or sociology, or economics, or philosophy, as its interpretative followers. Nor are any of these fields alone the necessary prior or initiating condition of knowledge. We all learn stories from each other—language takes its meaning from interaction. The scientist works with the ideal stories already available (hierarchy or simplicity, for example). Sometimes he or she adds a new one, or, more often, revises the imaginative meaning and explanatory power of an old one. The excitement generated among non-scientists by chaos theory is an instance: chaos theory calls attention to observed but excluded irregularity, asymmetry and flux. That it has developed alongside deconstruction, with its refusal of parameters of interpretation, its obdurate relativism, is as intriguing as is the re-discovery of plate-tectonics at the height of the fashion for Derridean epistemology, with its emphasis on ungrounding.

Are such analogies just a play of words? I do not believe so. But neither do I believe that it is possible to produce a stable causal sequence to account for these temporal relations. Alongside such proximities one can detail technical permitting factors. The need to drill deep for oil, and the development of the technology to do so; the development of computers and their capacity to record fractals; these are crucial explanatory factors in placing the moment of theory-precipitation. But the technical account does not drive out the inter-active account. There is no necessary competition between these explanatory forms. Loose accords have their significance too. Scientists and writers dwell in the land of the living where multiple epistemological systems interlock, overlap, contradict, and sustain our day-by-day choices.

At present we are again in a moment when scientists are accepting the risks of uncontrolled reception. Writing that had initially sought and required the autonomy of the specialist group is now rapidly and copiously re-interpreted by wider and diversified groups of writers and readers. Literature also, like scientific activity, is now very consciously working across an international system of intertextuality with novels and plays from many countries rapidly translated into English. This further extends the degree to which the English language bears the determining forces of many, and various, communities.

Such free reception is not likely to leave scientific problems intact within the expository terms already established by scientists. Rather, the transformed materials of scientific writing become involved in social and artistic questioning. That questioning is enacted sometimes at the level of semantics, sometimes of form or of broken story. Transformations and imbalances reveal as much as congruities. Such enquiry must not be subordinated to current demands in our society for pre-determined relevance, nor can its success be measured by discovering identity between the different domains. The questioning of meaning in (and across) science and literature needs to be sustained without seeking always reconciliation.

Joseph Bard Memorial Lecture

THE PENNY WHISTLE: THE PROBLEM OF WRITING STORIES FROM SHAKESPEARE

LEON GARFIELD FRSL

Read 18 May 1989
Beryl Bainbridge, FRSL, in the Chair

MY TITLE is, as you may have guessed, a reference to the inadequacy of the instrument to the task. I can assure you, from hard experience, that to convey anything at all of the richness of a Shakespeare play, in terms of mere story, is like trying to play the Ninth Symphony of Beethoven on a penny whistle. However skilled a performer may be upon his modest instrument, he is all too conscious that his rendering falls somewhat short of complete success. So why, you might ask, attempt it at all? The answer, quite simply, is for money. But then, as Johnson said, no man but a blockhead wrote except for money.

The process is quite straightforward. A publisher (shrewd fellows all!) knows that if the mere name, Shakespeare, can be legitimately utilised on the cover of a book, then that book will be ensured of a respectable sale. If not exactly snapped up, it will at least be thought-fully fingered and frequently purchased by school libraries and middle-class parents malevolently disposed towards birthdays and Christmas. So the publisher hires (again in Johnson's words) a harmless drudge to turn out something that, if not readable, will, at least, be printable. Thus a gap in his list is filled and, as Gertrude was advised, he will have assumed a virtue even if he has it not.* So the harmless drudge takes his money (or a third of it), and sets to work. At once he is appalled by the enormity of the task, and is only sustained in it by the hope that he will fail less ingloriously than his predecessors. Of which, since Charles and Mary Lamb, there have been hundreds.

Mostly, these are of a very high-minded nature. In 1828, Caroline Maxwell, in her introduction to The Juvenile Edition of Shakespeare adapted to the capacities of Youth, writes: 'The design of this, is to relate the story of each drama, in the most simple and easy style, and that, most likely to impress on the youthful mind a perfect recollection of the incidents of each piece; and to introduce in the course of the narratives, some of the most beautiful passages which each contains, for study or recitation.' She concludes by assuring the intending purchaser, 'that any incident, passage or even word that might be thought exceptionable by the strictest delicacy, is entirely omitted, and on no occasion has the fair purity of the youthful mind been for one moment forgot, in offering, and in selecting, these pages for their perusal.'

Although, at first, this seems a precaution verging on the impious, my wife pointed out that there might be something in it after all; and that, were our young football supporters not so fatally addicted to the reading of unexpurgated Shakespeare, was it not possible that there would be less trouble on the terraces?

But however laudable the intention, the results of applying such a method all too frequently ends in absurdity. It is impossible not to sympathise with the agonies of delicacy that Dr Bowdler and his sister, Henrietta, must have endured when they were confronted by Othello; but surely no one could applaud the result of their labours which, while ingeniously omitting 'as prime as goats, as hot as monkeys', left in Othello's maddened cry of 'Goats and monkeys!' to stand as, apparently, a lunatic aberration of the poet. Similarly, Caroline Maxwell, while boldly attempting Cymbeline, brings herself to record, albeit with averted eyes, the shocking fact that Iachimo conceals himself in Imogen's bedchamber, she discreetly avoids mentioning his observation of a mole on the sleeping Imogen's breast. Consequently, Posthumus's loss of faith in his wife's fidelity is made

---

*I do not here include my own pupblisher, who is a pillar of rectitude and adourned with all the virtues!

to rest entirely on the evidence of a pilfered bracelet; which not only encourages a poor opinion of Posthumus's good sense, but also suggests that Iachimo, as a plotter, was optimistic to the point of idiocy.

Other re-tellings have ranged from the maddeningly cosy and avuncular, such as the writer introducing the colossal drama of Macbeth by confiding in his readers that there were once witches in Scotland and, for all he knows, they are still there; to the insanely academic in which, with an imposing display of learning, the reader is treated to an extensive topography of Classical Greece before being conducted, sedately, to a wood near Athens and A Midsummer Night's Dream.

Of course, when I browsed among these, my predecessors, I smiled indulgently at their many inadequacies; that is, until I settled down to make the attempt myself. And then I discovered that it was very much a case of 'when sorrows come, they come not single spies, but in battalions.' And I was tempted to throw up the task in despair.

At the outset, my greatest difficulty was to overcome my sense of awe; for, as Caroline Spurgeon wisely observed, 'No one can study Shakespeare closely for years without being reduced to a condition of complete humility.'

But I very soon discovered that too much respect can be as damaging as too little. However wonderful a passage, too lengthy an extract from it, even by so much as a single line, can slow down a narrative disastrously and so give a totally false impression of a drama that, on the stage, proceeds at a tremendous pace. So, however heart-breaking, sacrifices had to be made for the good of the whole; and I can assure you that Jeptha never sacrificed his daughter with half the regret with which I, after having typed, 'Our revels now are ended,' followed it with an ellipsis so that the conspiracy of Caliban and his companions might be brought to confusion before the reader had forgotten all about it.

But of course, however much quotation may be curtailed, it would be absured to do without it entirely. Quite apart from Caroline Maxwell's laudable intention of including beautiful passages for the purpose of study or recitation, it is necessary to make use of it as dialogue. Every story is enlivened by dialogue. It both regulates the pace of the narrative, and ventilates the look of the page. Nothing is more daunting to the unwilling reader (and, to the storyteller, every reader must be deemed to be unwilling), than an unending acreage of solid print with nothing but the occasional paragraph to provide a little oasis of excitement or relief. Now having decided that dialogue is necessary, nobody but a fool would waste his time in inventing it when he can pillage from the best there is. It would be like offering your dinner guests home grown cabbage when you could have regaled them with asparagus, growing plentifully in the public domain. But once you quote, and I mean in the way of using Shakespeare's lines as natural speech, you are in trouble. As Logan Pearsall Smith once wrote: 'the mere gleam of a Shakespearian phrase lights up with a sudden illumination the alien page on which I find it.'

So now I come to the third problem: language. The direct speech should never look out of place; which means that the prose that surrounds it should approximate to it, if not in quality, then at least in cadence and vocabulary. This, in my case, has meant extensive use of Schmidt's Shakespeare Lexicon and a Concordance of such impressive dimensions that I am still limping from having dropped it on my foot while trying to find the world, 'preposterous'.

Although this means a great deal more work, it is, I feel, justified; to use modern vocabulary to describe the actions of Shakespeare's characters is apt to produce the same disjointed effect as does a performance in modern dress, of which Harley Granville-Barker once wrote: 'It may be a purge and a tonic to the sluggish-fancied spectator to be shown a Prince of Denmark in coat and trousers and a Grave-digger in a bowler hat, for reminder that here is a play and not a collection of ritualized quotations. But physic is for the sick . . .'

I know that it was, and quite possibly still is, fashionable to point out that the plays were originally performed in a roughly contemporary costume; but then, so was the language; and to up-date the one and not (please God!) the other, has the effect of distancing the verse rather than making it more immediate. I remember seeing a Romeo and Juliet—or at least the first half of it—in which Tybalt fought with a flick knife and a bicycle chain and the guests at the Capulet's ball plunged, shrieking with laughter, into a modest-sized swimming pool. I left during the interval because I could not for a moment believe in a sweatshirt and jean-clad Romeo being capable of anything more eloquent than a rudimentary grunting, let alone Renaissance blank verse; and his death, so far as I was concerned, was likely to be too long delayed.

Now although Shakespeare's vocabulary is enormous, not ever stepping outside it bristles with difficulties. Many a time, in the dull, leaden heat of composition, a word has occurred to me that seems precisely right. It describes exactly what I want, neither more nor less. Then, an uneasy feeling comes over me. I consult Schmidt and, sure enough, my worst fears are realised: the word is not there. Result: fury and frustration, and yet another page in the waste-paper basket. (I do not use a word-processor; I find the business of writing hard enough as it is, without having my words flung back in my face from an illuminated screen.) Then, little by little, the despair diminishes, and second, third and even fourth thoughts succeed one another and produce, in the end, something far superior to the first. More often than not, that first word, which would have filled the bill so admirably, gives way to a piece of imagery that is infinitely more vivid. Indeed, I have found it perfectly possible to write within Shakespeare's vocabulary without being in the least archaic; and, what is more, I have found the exercise has done nothing but good for my prose. I think that Dr Abbott, in his Shakespearian Grammar, sums it up wonderfully well when he says: 'We may perhaps claim some superiority in completeness and perspicuity for modern English, but if we were to appeal on this ground to the shade of Shakespeare in the words of Antonio in The Tempest: 'Do you not hear us speak?' we might fairly be crushed with the reply of Sebastian: 'I do; and surely it is a sleepy language.'

Yet another problem which, although it applies to the telling of the story of any play, is peculiarly acute with Shakespeare; it is the problem of viewpoint. To take the viewpoint of the author is manifestly impossible. We simply don't know it. To take the viewpoint of a principal character is only permissable when he reveals himself in soliloquy. Sometimes it is possible to take the viewpoint of a secondary character who is present in a scene and whose feelings are affected by what he observes. But most often the best viewpoint to take is that of a deeply attentive audience whose imagination has indeed 'turned the accomplishment of many years into an hourglass' and 'into a thousand parts divided one man.'

There was such an audience once, an audience such as any playwright must dream of it. It was that famous audience in the American West in the last century. A touring theatrical company was presenting Othello, and the actor playing Iago was giving so convincing a performance that a member of the audience, outraged by his monstrous villainy, got up and shot him dead. One can only hope that divine justice allowed that actor, before he expired, time enough to savour in full the extent of his triumph, and that, when he arrived in Heaven, Shakespeare shook him by the hand.

The method I have adopted in my own re-tellings has been to remember, as best I can, various performances I have seen and to attempt to convey an impression of them—not so much as stage plays but as actual dramas. In other words, I have tried to produce the plays on the printed page, with all the advantages and disadvantages that that entails. For instance, I can create, in a paragraph, a far more convincing storm than any stage could supply; but I cannot begin to do justice to Lear's frantic utterances in the way a fine actor can. So, rather than destroy what it is my intention to promote, I leave out the poetry and concentrate on the stage carpentry.

I prefer, always, to think of performances I have seen a long time ago, as I find it fatal to rely on too recent an experience. I remember being hugely impressed by a performance of The Comedy of Errors that I saw, in of all places, Amsterdam. It was performed by what was virtually a street theatre and it was so swift and energetic that I was completely captivated by it; and straightway attempted the re-telling of that particular play. The result, after some six weeks of work, was, to say the least of it, dull, flat and unprofitable. It was a disaster. I had lost the essence in a too vivid recollection of detail.

Of course, I should have known better. Past experience of my own work should have taught me. I have always found that, in the writing of any piece of fiction, if I wanted to convey the feeling of a place that I had known in childhood, the very worst thing I could do was to go and visit it again. Such a course of action, far from being helpful, kills the imagination . . . which, when all is said and done, is little more than looking at memory through half-closed eyes. But then nobody ever really profits from experience; all we seem to do is to keep up the payments.

There are, of course, countless difficulties other than those I have spoken of, that have confronted me as I have laboured through some dozen of the plays; so now, if you will bear with me, I will take you through one of them—the most recent with which I have been wrestling—in an effort to show how I have attempted to overcome its many, and often unexpected problems. The play was Julius Caesar, a play that ought not to have presented the difficulties of, say, Henry IV Part One. It is, on the face of it, a straightforward, vigorous drama, unencumbered by sub-plots and written in Shakespeare's plainest style. It has a smaller vocabulary than almost any other of

Shakespeare's plays. This, and a large number of short lines have led some scholars to question its authorship and maintain that the play we have represents a revision of what Shakespeare wrote by other, inferior hands. However, most scholars, I am happy to say, warmly disagree, and many a fair reputation lies bleeding among the footnotes. But, although fascinating, I have never found such quibbling scholarship helpful. I prefer to read those commentaries that award unstinting praise, as it is important for me to believe whole-heartedly in the superiority of the play I am engaged upon. Each in turn, must be the best; whether it be King Lear or Love's Labours Lost. And it is not so very difficult. After all, who but a fool, standing among the foothills, would disparage K2 because he has been told that Everest is loftier. Both are in the clouds.

But to return to Julius Caesar. It opens, I need hardly remind you—but I will all the same!—with the happy excitement of a holiday being violently opposed by the tribunes, Flavius and Marellus, who, although they are named, I preferred to introduce as two officers of state, partly because the reader, in all likelihood, won't know what a tribune is, and it will worry him, and partly because, in a narrative of some eight thousand words, it is best to restrict names to the chief protagonists, to avoid confusion. And then there is the all-important crowd . . . or the common people, or the unruly throng, or the multitude . . . anything, in short, except the one word that springs to mind: the mob. Unhappily, the word mob, in the sense of a riotous assembly, was not in use until the early eighteenth century. But I found it was possible to do without it. Sometimes, even, the lack of the word proved to be a positive advantage, such as when, to avoid repetition, I was forced into the longer, but, I think, far better: 'all the cobblers and carpenters and tradesmen and their wives . . .' That, I felt, had at least the merit of picturing the crowd, rather than merely referring to it. The entry of Caesar, with all the great ones of Rome following, like faithful dogs, provides an ideal opportunity to introduce the chief characters in a natural manner, and to add, for good measure, old Cicero, toddling along as if his new sandals pinched —thus emphasising the festive nature of the occasion.

The only indication of a scene (and that, supplied by a later editor), is Rome. A Street. I preferred to use the market-place, which gave me space enough to relate the whole of the first act without slowing down the action to describe a different location. Also, it enabled me to conceal my total ignorance of the topography of Ancient Rome.

But far and away the most formidable problem in the opening scenes, was to show the greatness of Caesar; for unless Caesar is seen to be a colossal figure, the assassination loses its importance. I toyed with the idea, that some stage directors have used, of having a gigantic statue of Caesar, with arm outstretched as if across the world, dominating the market-place. This would have given me the advantage of contrasting the stone Caesar with the living man, Caesarism with Caesar. But, at the same time, it would have reduced the living man to a strutting pigmy; which he most certainly was not. So, however tempting it was to play with the fascinating possibility of the principal characters vanishing in the huge shadow, I reluctantly abandoned it and decided—my mind still running on statuary—to furnish the market place with marble Romans of the Republic, clutching their scrolls of liberty. Then, when Caesar approached, they could conceivably turn pale and clutch their scrolls more tightly, as if they feared a thief was about.

And so, after the dramatic intervention of 'Beware the Ides of March' and Caesar's magnificent reply of, 'He is a dreamer. Let us leave him. Pass.' to Brutus and Cassius.

This is the first intimate scene, and it is chiefly Cassius's; so Brutus is to be observed through Cassius's eyes. It is a scene of extraordinary subtlety and almost impossible to convey, short of quoting it in its entirety. But then one might say the same of the whole play, abandon the typewriter, present the publisher with the Arden edition and return the advance. I can assure you that, many a time I have been tempted to follow that course; but, so far, I have managed to restrain the impulse, partly because of a natural reluctance to return money, but mostly because of a very real wish to provide an acceptable introduction to the plays. But to return to the great scene of the temptation of Brutus. The only solution I could find was in the use of imagery. Fortunately Cassius himself provides the image when he says: 'I am glad that my weak words have struck but thus much show of fire from Brutus.' Consequently I felt free to describe Cassius and Brutus murmuring together, 'the one tall and upright, the other, slighter and fiercely restless, like a darting flame striving to set a mighty tree ablaze.'

Another image that I found helpful to impose on the scene was that of Cassius playing on Brutus's sense of honour as if it was an instrument. Not my own image, as for a few intoxicating moments I thought it was, but, as I'm sure you all remember, borrowed from

Hamlet. But then, as Keats said, Shakespeare left nothing to be said about nothing or everything. And how brilliantly Cassius does play on that instrument! When he says, 'Why, man, he doth bestride the narrow world like a colossus, and we *petty* men walk under his huge legs and peep about to find ourselves *dishonourable* graves!' how Brutus must have flinched at those words! They must have been like dagger thrusts! And yet I have never seen an actor react as I feel he should; but then, being an actor, he is probably not listening, but merely waiting for his cue line to burst in with something of his own.

At this point it is tempting to speculate on Brutus. How much had he thought privately about toppling Caesar? Is his parade of honour no more than a cloak for personal ambition? But it would be unwise to do more than speculate. Brutus must always be as Shakespeare shows him; and to try to follow him, and pry into his thoughts when he is not on stage would amount to imposing a personal opinion on the reader rather than letting him indulge in surmises for himself. At all times, the expression, 'he thought that', should be avoided, as it infallibly breaks the illusion of the reality of the play. I try to keep a strict judge inside my head who is quick to say, 'Confine yourself to the evidence and spare us your opinions.'

The remainder of the scene presented no great problems, and the storm scene that follows it provided me with a welcome opportunity for some extravagant stage-carpentry. I enjoyed it thoroughly . . . that is, until I realised that it was really a prophetic image of the storms to follow; in particular, the violent uprising set into motion by Mark Antony; so that the storm images needed to be carefully controlled so they might be related to the action of the crowd.

In order to preserve the continuity of action, I linked the two scenes together by, I admit, an entirely unauthorised use of the Soothsayer. I kept him in the market-place so that, when the conspirators had departed, he was able to stare after them ominously. This not only produced a sense of foreboding, but also gave me the opportunity to remind the reader of the Ides of March and inform him that they were to be on the very next day.

This, I find, is always a problem in story-telling; the problem of how much can the reader's memory be relied upon? Not for much more than a couple of pages, I suspect; and it is a suspicion that can readily be confirmed by watching how often a reader frowns and riffles back through pages in search of that necessary piece of information in the previous chapter that quite escaped him.

The scene in Brutus's orchard moves at a slower tempo; (how often Shakespeare sets scenes of great inwardness in orchards!) but it is a scene from which scarcely anything can be omitted without undermining the plot. There is Brutus's false reasoning for the necessity of Caesar's death; there is the meeting of the conspirators during which Antony is mentioned for the first time as a figure of importance; and, above all, there is the wonderful scene with Portia, which, although not strictly necessary to the plot, is vital to the emotional force of play. My chief problem was how to include my favourite lines without overburdening the narrative. Eventually, apart from a few conversational exchanges, I had to settle for no more than Portia's 'Am I your self but, as it were, in sort or limitation, to keep with you at meals, comfort your bed, and talk to you sometimes? Dwell I but in the suburbs of your good pleasure?' Not very much, perhaps, but enough, I felt, for even the most carping critic to concede some merit, if nowhere else, at least in the dialogue!

Now the tempo quickens again. The scene with Portia pleading with Brutus is marvellously paralleled by the scene of Calpurnia pleading with Caesar. The events are moving swiftly towards the murder. There is a brief scene in which Portia displays her terrible anxiety for her husband. At first, I was tempted to omit it; but then I realised that a single scene for Portia was not enough if her death was to have the required effect on Brutus. So I included it; and, in doing so, came upon one of those extraordinary touches that Shakespeare manages so effortlessly. He seems to have time for everything, and yet never distorts the shape of the play. This ability, must come from a complete grasp of the construction. In a lesser way, one notices this ability in the manner in which a great interpreter, like say, Maria Callas, appears to vary the pace within a musical phrase without ever destroying the basic tempo. The touch I was referring to is when Portia, at her wit's end to find an excuse for sending her servant to her husband, tells him to tell Brutus that she is merry. At first sight, this is little more than a touching revelation of Portia's agitated state of mind: that is, until one remembers that, only a little while before, Brutus, when bidding farewell to the conspirators, warned them not to betray themselves by their pale looks. 'Gentlemen,' he urged them, 'look fresh and merrily.' Then one realises the full significance of Portia's message; and one sits back with a gasp of admiration.

And so to the assassination itself . . . or rather, to the terrifying

moments before it. Here again, was the problem of viewpoint. I felt
that to take the view of the audience would necessitate moving from
character to character in a way that would lessen the tension. To take
the view of either Cassius or Brutus would mean entering their minds
in a wholly inappropriate way. Besides, I found it impossible to
imagine what they might be thinking. To take the view of Caesar
himself was plainly unprofitable as, very shortly, he was to be
deprived of any point of view at all. So I decided to make use of a
secondary character with whose fate the reader would not be deeply
concerned. I chose Casca, because he was to strike the first blow; and
it was not hard to imagine the emotions of such a man at such a time. I
conceived him as being absolutely terrified and presented him, 'with
his right hand hidden in his gown, walking as if on egg-shells and
sweating like an actor fearful of mangling his part.'

Everything was prepared. Casca had moved round to the back of
Caesar's chair. The conspirators were kneeling. The blow was about
to fall . . . when I came across a footnote, or, rather, a riot of
footnotes. I left Brutus, Cassius and the rest of them where they were,
eyes bulging and hands on knives, while I pursued, as avidly as a
hungry dog, the footnotes. I had reached, I discovered, a disputed
passage. It concerned the tremendous moment when Metellus Cim-
ber, kneeling before Caesar, is pleading abjectly for the repeal of his
brother's banishment. Caesar rejects the plea contemptuously, and
ends with, 'I spurn thee like a cur out of my way. Know, Caesar doth
not wrong, nor without cause will he be satisfied.' The controversy has
its origin with Ben Jonson, who, after having praised Shakespeare,
wrote that, 'Many times he fell into those things could not escape
laughter: as when he said, in the person of Caesar, one speaking to
him, 'Caesar thou dost me wrong,' he replied, 'Caesar did never
wrong, but with just cause'; and suchlike; which were ridiculous.' It
has been assumed that either Jonson altered the passage before it was
printed, or Shakespeare, in deference to Jonson's opinion, made the
change himself. Either way, I find the version that Jonson laughed at
to be stronger than the reading in the Folio. 'Caesar did never wrong,
but with just cause,' seems to me a piece of biting irony totally in
keeping with the play. I spent a week, trying to find a commentator
who agreed with me. The best I could find was Arthur Humphreys'
concession that the earlier version had the merit of eliminating
a half line. That was enough for me. I was determined to use
it. But, unfortunately, when I returned to the conspirators, I felt

that they had been waiting quite long enough without my holding up the action further, for however scholarly a reason. So I left it out.

And so, at last, to the murder. Mankiewicz, in his splendid film, has Caesar standing, and huddled about by the conspirators, which, I felt, although simple to describe, gave the action too furtive an air. In view of Brutus's determination that the killing should be a sacrificial act, I felt that a more overtly theatrical a setting was needed, a setting more in keeping with the strange scene that follows, and Cassius's 'How many ages hence shall this our lofty scene be acted o'er.' Caesar must be seated in his chair of state, with the senators, seated in a great semi-circle before him, like an audience at a play. Then, and only then, can the hideous butchery of the killing be contrasted with the stately ceremony that precedes it. For the actual amplification of the Folio's stage direction of, They stab Caesar, and, Dies, I turned to Shakespeare's own source, Plutarch, which, I felt sure, must have been followed when the play was first staged. It is a truly terrifying scene, in which the conspirators wound one another in their mad haste to stick their knives into Caesar. I confess, with a certain degree of shame, that it was a hugely enjoyable scene to write; and I found myself thinking, not without a pang of regret, how very different from our own House of Commons.

The scene that follows—the horrified silence, broken by Cinna's cry of, 'Liberty! Freedom! Tyranny is dead!' and then the rushing away of the senators, presented my usual semantic difficulty. The word that most readily comes to mind to describe the mood of the onlookers is, of course, panic. But unfortunately the word panic, in the sense of extreme fear, was not in use until about a hundred years later. Fear, dread, horror and terror were all words that had either already occurred in too close a context, or else were not strong enough. So once again I had recourse to imagery; and, bearing in mind that the predominant imagery of the play is animal imagery, and that, as Caroline Spurgeon noted, Shakespeare's images are mostly of a homely, domestic nature, I arrived at this. 'There was an uproar of overturned chairs and stumbling feet as the terrified senators, squealing like chickens rushing from the axe, fled from the men of blood.'

Then comes Antony. Now although the holding back of a principal character until halfway through the play—for up until this moment he has spoken barely half a dozen lines—did not seem to present the playwright with any difficulty, it does to the storyteller. There is so little space in which to establish him without slowing down the forward movement; for it would be fatal, at this point, to interrupt the rush of events towards the great Forum scene and the riot of the crowd. So the most that I could do to suggest the masker and reveller of Cassius's contemptuous description was to have him enter with an unsteady gait and eyes still looped with shadows. Not nearly enough, but then I hoped to find space later, at some time when a larger description would seem more natural and, preferably, given through another character's eyes.

The Forum scene itself presents any re-teller of Shakespeare (as, indeed, it must to any actor), with an insuperable problem: how to launch a speech that is almost too famous, and make it seem a perfectly natural utterance.

'To be, or not to be,' in Hamlet presents the problem in its most acute form. I remember, when I made what I consider to be a valiant attempt at that play, that I was sorely tempted to omit the speech altogether. After all, I thought, Hamlet is rich enough without it. But in the end I managed to devise a method of introducing it in a way that I felt satisfied the demands of storytelling without putting the reader out of all patience. Traditionally, and I think it a good tradition, Hamlet enters reading a book. But what book, and why? These are questions that any storyteller might reasonably ask. What more likely, then, that he should be reading his own commonplace book, the very 'tables' in which he set down his feelings on his first encounter with the ghost? The why can be answered plainly enough. Surely the reason lies in his previous soliloquy, in which he questioned the veracity of the ghost. In other words, he is searching for that entry, when, quite by chance, he comes upon his notes of an old lecture in Wittenburg; for, 'To be, or not to be', is very much in the manner of a professor putting a problem forward for debate. So Hamlet reads it with an air of a musing reminiscence, and, only later in the speech does he look up and continue as the debate's substance finds an echo in his own condition.

To such extremes is one driven in such a task of storytelling! While not presenting quite so severe a problem as to be or not to be, Antony's 'Friends, Romans, countrymen', was almost equally difficult to launch. Taking into account the circumstances, not so much of the stage, when the actor commands silence by his presence and doubt-less, the instructions of the producer, but of the written story when a vast crowd, having been wildly excited by the speech of Brutus, is in no mood to listen to yet another speech (and how we sympathise!) it is hard to imagine how Antony can make himself heard. Certainly not by merely shouting. However powerful his voice, it would hardly drown out the hubbub of half Rome. And yet he must command attention. This, I felt, could only be realistically achieved in the way a skilled [and selfish] actor gains attention by some small, but shrewdly calculated piece of stage business. He might blow his nose, look out of a window, or even scratch his head. If he judges it right, the audience instantly turns to watch him, and ignores whatever else might be taking place on the stage. So Antony, having tried twice to gain a hearing, and having twice failed, and needing something a little more noteworthy than the flourishing of a pocket handkerchief, looks about him. As luck, in this case, the storyteller, would have it, he sees that, from the sheeted-over body of Caesar, lying on its bier, an arm has slipped and is hanging down. Instantly he goes to lift it up, kisses the dead hand, and lays it reverently on Caesar's breast. That, I felt, *would* command attention; and once he has it, he never lets it go.

But still Antony is incomplete. So far, there has been neither time nor place to show the masker and the reveller . . . so necessary as a preparation for the later Antony of Antony and Cleopatra. But I found the opportunity in the very next scene: that chilling scene when Antony, Lepidus and Octavius sit over their list of senators and prick them down for death. The scene, as you may remember, takes place in Antony's house; so it was possible to show both the other Antony and the highly unpleasant, accountant-like figure of Octavius at one and the same time. I visualised the cold, precise young man looking round with some distaste at the empty bottles and faded remembrances of ladies that undoubtedly littered Antony's room.

A minor triumph, I felt; but disaster lay directly ahead. The quarrel scene between Brutus and Cassius; a marvellous scene, and one of the very greatest that Shakespeare ever wrote. No quotation could possibly do it justice, nor could any imagery hope to encompass the fury of emotions that the scene expresses. The best I could do was to liken it to the assassination itself, in which Caesar's friends hacked and stabbed him to death; for that is what Brutus seems to be doing to Cassius. Indeed, Cassius himself is driven to beg Brutus to kill him, even as he killed Caesar; so perhaps the image was not entirely inappropriate after all.

The scene leads to Brutus's anguished confiding in Cassius of

Portia's death. Now here there is controversy. You can always tell when it is upon you: two lines of verse, and the rest of the page, footnotes! The controversy is because the revelation of Portia's death occurs twice: once when Brutus tells Cassius in private, and, immediately after when Messala, who has news of his own from Rome, tells Brutus in the presence of others; and Brutus, accepting the news as if for the first time, displays a true Roman fortitude with an almost casual, 'Why, farewell, Portia.' It has been suggested that Shakespeare originally wrote the second, Roman version, and then, finding it an inadequate requiem for the wonderful figure he had created in Portia, substituted the second, longer and more deeply felt farewell; and that either he or the printer neglected to cancel the other. There is absolutely no evidence for this, and the controversy rests entirely on the taste and preference of various editors and producers. Many authorities advocate cutting the second revelation as, they feel, it shows Brutus in a highly questionable light . . . which the whole tenor of the play strongly contradicts. For my part, I was, at first, inclined to follow their advice and leave Portia with a single farewell; but, just as earlier, I had found it necessary to include Portia's second brief scene, in order for her to make her full effect, so I now found it to be necessary to include the second farewell, in order to express more fully, Brutus's grief. In fact, when I read and re-read the scene, I came to thinking that the second, Roman farewell, was even more moving than the first. And it seemed so right. After all, Brutus is a man who would shrink from pity. After the first revelation, when he has reluctantly opened his heart to Cassius, his servant enters and Brutus hurriedly begs Cassius to say no more of his loss. And then again, when Messala and Titinius enter, and Cassius, still shocked, says, 'Portia, art thou gone?' Brutus again begs him to say no more. So that when Messala gives him the news, he cannot bear to say that he already knows, for fear of pity, and his Roman fortitude is no more than an iron mask, which by its very rigidity, repels any extravagant display of sympathy and stifles pity before it can be expressed.

So now to the last act, which some have criticized as being a falling-off, while others have declared it to be a masterpiece of construction. Needless to say, I myself took the latter view.

At the very outset, there is the tremendous confrontation before the battle, between Brutus and Cassius and Antony and Octavius in which they hurl insults at each other; and which, I find the most memorable part to be Antony's response to Cassius's jeering, 'A peevish schoolboy joined with a masker and a reveller.' All he says is, 'Old Cassius still!' What a world of feeling there is in those three words, uttered at such a time! Suddenly Antony the brilliant opportunist, Antony the ruthless politician, becomes Antony, the man of sentiment. For, however you say those words, 'Old Cassius still!' it is impossible not to say them without affection. It is very plain that, at that moment, Antony must feel that he has more in common with Cassius than with the cold young man by his side.

Then there are the immensely moving farewells of Cassius and Brutus; and so solemn are they that any reader, even though he might be ignorant of what is to come, must feel that their end is near and the battle is as good as lost. But even now, Shakespeare is by no means at the end of his resources, even though I was very nearly at the end of mine. He had time for three suicides; I, alas, could only manage one. Cassius's death I dealt with in retrospect, and Titinius's, not at all. I needed the space to do some sort of justice to Brutus's end. In particular, I wanted to bring Strato before the reader. Here is another of Shakespeare's miracles. Strato, who has not appeared before and, when Brutus is asking his friends, one by one, if they will help him to kill himself, is fast asleep. With Shakespeare, sleep seems synonymous with innocence and goodness. So it is Strato, a plain, not very bright soldier, who stays behind when the others have gone and holds the sword for Brutus to run upon. But first he demands, 'Give me your hand first,' And when the victors arrive, Strato is still there to say proudly, 'I held the sword, and he did run on it.' Strato seems to express Brutus's honour uncorrupted by philosophy and thought.

The last words of the play are given to Octavius, as they are in Antony and Cleopatra. The accountant always wins. But before that, there is Antony's fine tribute over the dead Brutus, culminating in, 'His life was gentle, and the elements so mixed up in him that Nature might stand up and say to all the world, "This was a man!"'

At this point, I found it impossible not to imagine Antony glancing sideways at Octavius, and slightly shaking his head. I took this small liberty partly because I disliked Octavius so much, and partly because I wanted to pave the way for the Antony who was next to be seen in the arms of Cleopatra.

And so I came to the end of my pilgrimage. At every step of the way I tried not to depart from my first intention, which was to be true to the play, and always to seek to bring my readers to Shakespeare, rather than Shakespeare to my readers. The best success I could have would be for my story to make my readers wish to both see and to read the play. Wearily, then, I closed all the editions that lay scattered over my desk, and tucked thirty-three pages of typescript into an expensive folder, the gift of my daughter; not with any sensation of achievement, I can assure you, but with the distinct feeling that I had identified myself rather too closely with Brutus and Cassius, and had, like them, murdered Julius Caesar.

Tredegar Memorial Lecture

THE OTHER JANE AUSTEN: NON-REALIST ELEMENTS IN HER FICTION

GILBERT PHELPS FRSL

Read 16 March 1989
John Press, FRSL, in the Chair

Is THERE anything new to be said about Jane Austen? One has the feeling that any attempt to do so is almost an act of sacrilege, as if one were desecrating some eighteenth century garden whose lay-out is sacrosanct. Many writers have been enclosed and to some extent diminished by the cult that has grown up around them, and perhaps this is especially the case with Jane Austen.

My title speaks of 'Non-Realist Elements' in Jane Austen's fiction. The term 'Realism', of course, begs all sorts of questions, and I'm not going to get entangled here in all the complex aesthetic and epistemological thickets. What I *do* want to argue is that there are elements in Jane Austen's novels for which the label 'realist', as the term is commonly understood, is only partially appropriate. I believe that much more breaks through that celebrated control, reticence and precision—terms which have become almost clichés of Jane Austen criticism—than is sometimes allowed, that this comes from the subconscious part of her creativity, and that it surfaces from time to time in narrative patterns and devices, symbolic episodes, and highly-charged words and phrases which are the reverse of realistic in the narrower sense of the term. To put it in a more fashionably 'modernist' way, in Jane Austen's fiction there is often what amounts to an exciting and mysterious sub-text.

In *Northanger Abbey* (assuming this to have been her first novel, though it wasn't published until 1818, after her death) she was disposing of the Gothic Novel and the Novel of Sensibility—aberrations which threatened to divert the English Novel from its proper course—and *Sense and Sensibility* (1811) was to some extent a continuation of the demolition process as far as the second of these genres was concerned. In neither case, however, was it a simple matter of poking fun. Even these early novels contain features which go beyond the crude popular image of Jane Austen as predominantly a witty social satirist of a straightforward 'realistic' kind. I am not, of course, in any way decrying the 'realism' of Jane Austen's own nature, her commonsense approach with its calls for 'what is simple and probable' and for the 'natural' as opposed to the 'heroic', calls which cut through the falsities engendered by over-romantic fantasy fiction. I certainly wouldn't wish to minimise her great comic gifts either. But I think that some redistribution of emphases is necessary. There is already a good deal in *Northanger Abbey*, in fact, that is *not* consonant either with reality to life, or to the kind of fiction that purports to reflect it—and nothing certainly that could be called 'naturalistic' in the documentary sense.

There is, to begin with, a very characteristic stylisation and formal patterning: the symmetrical arrangement of pairs of siblings, for example—in this case Isabella and James Thorpe on the one hand, and Henry and Eleanor Tilney on the other—the heroine's false friends as opposed to her genuine ones. There is the equally characteristic use of the ballroom as a paradigm of the dance of the sexes; Henry Tilney in fact makes the point when he says: 'I consider a country dance as an emblem of marriage. Fidelity and complaisance are the principal duties of both'. There is the use of Bath as a microcosm of the 'world', which Catherine must enter—and when she and Henry climb to the topmost crescent, the panorama of the city is laid out before her, almost as if it were a Temptation, and what must be stressed is that this isn't a mere exercise in topographical exactitude: the highways and byways of Bath also represent the heroine's own inner journeyings. For the real subject of all Jane Austen's novels is the process of psychological and spiritual reformation taking place within the heroine's inner world. Everything else is subordinated to that ruling purpose, and that includes if need be, plot and even characterisation, and always there are episodes which aren't strictly consistent with the processes of cause and effect, though in her later fiction she was more adept at concealing the fact. In *Northanger Abbey* they do rather stick out. Henry Tilney, for instance, begins as something of a connoisseur of the Gothic and the Picturesque, but is later the chief agent in debunking them; his father, the General, doesn't seem to be the same man in the middle of the novel as he was at the beginning, and he changes again before the end.

But Jane Austen doesn't care overmuch about such inconsistencies: her overriding concern is to forward her heroine's inner exploration. Admittedly there is a paradox here, in that the end to be achieved is the weaning of the heroine from her illusions and misconceptions about herself and her place in the world, so that she accepts *its reality*: but the means whereby Jane Austen brings this about are *not* realistic in the usual sense. She was not, of course, an allegorist like John Bunyan: she preferred to make use of the ready-to-hand materials of the English Novel as she found it—but her methods are often closer to allegory than to realism. She is, first and foremost, an artist who creates her own world with its own laws and conventions.

As for *Sense and Sensibility*, the patterning is almost too schematic. This is most obvious in the title itself, and in the *apparent* balancing of the two sisters, with Elinor *apparently* standing for Sense, and Marianne for Sensibility. In fact these oppositions are nothing like as crude as this would suggest. For one thing, even at the start the sisters do not present a simple dualism. It is true that Elinor knows how to control her feelings, while Marianne does not. It is also probable that Jane Austen's ostensible purpose was to demonstrate the dangers of the kind of emotional liberation advocated by Jean Jacques Rousseau and the Romantics, as against the merits of restraint and decorum in the service of the earlier 18th c. ideal of a well-ordered society. But Jane Austen's attitude towards the two sisters is a decidedly ambivalent one, and there is a tension in the novel between the opposing claims of sense and sensibility which is far from simple in any diagrammatic way, and which results in images, verbal usages, and incidents that are symbolic in a fundamentally poetic sense, besides reaching to a level of psychological profundity beyond anything previously achieved in the English Novel.

For one thing the sisters change. Marianne acquires more sense while Elinor acquires more sensibility. This is the point in Elinor's case of that extraordinary episode when Willoughby dashes up to the house, where Marianne is lying ill, to make his confession to Elinor. 'A blunder that cannot be condoned' accordingly to George Moore, but we are not dealing with the requirements of naturalistic verisimilitude, and this is one of Jane Austen's emblematic scenes, focusing the moral issues, in which Elinor finds it in her heart, after Willoughby has gone, to murmur 'poor Willoughby' and to feel a 'pang' for him.

One of the unspoken reasons for the softening of Elinor's heart is that she is in some respects a fellow-victim—of the pressures exerted by a society in which it is more 'sensible' for Willoughby to have married his heiress rather than the penniless Marianne, and which is so devastatingly illustrated by the dreadful Dashwoods and the equally despicable Ferrars family. Willoughby of course deserves what he gets: but those decent characters who try to fulfil their inner selves within the dictates of their kind of society must suffer intensely. This is just as true of Elinor as of Marianne. She is the one who tries to mediate, for her sister's sake as well as her own, between the claims of emotion and those of society, but time after time she nearly cracks under the strain. When, for example, Lucy Steele hints at the understanding between herself and Edward Ferrars, Elinor is seized by 'an emotion and distress beyond anything she had ever felt'. There is no lack of passionate feeling here. The difference between Elinor and Marianne is that the former only gives way to her feelings in private, while the latter despises concealment. But although Jane Austen may have been advocating Elinor's strategy, she is far from dismissing Marianne's behaviour as that of a silly love-sick girl who has read too many novels of sensibility. Her sufferings, too, are real, as witness the muffled scream of anguish she utters in London, and the illness which nearly kills her after Willoughby's betrayal, to which the modern term 'psychosomatic' can so obviously be applied.

It seems clear to me that there was as much of Marianne as of Elinor in Jane Austen's own nature. More of Marianne perhaps than she cared to admit, which may explain why she marries her off to Colonel Brandon at the end of the novel, as if she didn't quite know what to do with her—leaving us with a feeling that Marianne's surrender to 'sense' has left her somehow impoverished. It would have been artistically truer, we sometimes feel, if Jane Austen had left Marianne die. For potentially *Sense and Sensibility is* a tragic novel about the clash of irreconcilable forces and the inevitability of crippling frustration in a materialistic, paternalistic and repressive society where rigid 'forms' and conventions play too great a part. In Jane Austen's time it was of course the women who were the main sufferers—and I am surprised that (as far as I know) feminist criticism has never seized upon *Sense and Sensibility* as one of its most illuminating texts.

The force of Jane Austen's own imaginative and emotional involvement with these strains and tensions had the effect of extruding elements which have more in common with poetry or poetic drama than with conventional Realism. This is apparent in the use of key ideas, words and phrases which, in the context of the novel, take on a peculiar potency. There are, for example, frequent references to concealment and secrecy, as well as a proliferation of actual secrets —such as Colonel Brandon's in connection with Eliza and her mother, and the secret of Lucy's engagement to Edward, all of them not merely conducive to the conduct of the plot, but also symbolically symptomatic of rigid social forms driving the natural life of the emotions underground. Even the eminently honest Elinor is forced into polite evasions in order to survive. In her case a key image is that of screens—at the party in London where Willoughby so cruelly snubs Marianne, for instance, Elinor attempts to 'screen' her sister's agitation from the onlookers, and it is significant that one of her 'accomplishments' is the making of actual screens.

The most striking symbolic illustration of repressed emotion, though, belongs not to Elinor or Marianne but to Edward, who has, we are told, lived a life of '*fettered* inclination', because of his parents' social ambitions for him. When eventually he is free to seek out Elinor, in his nervousness 'He rose from his seat and walked to the window, apparently not knowing what to do; took up a pair of scissors that lay there . . . spoiling both them and their sheath by cutting the latter to pieces as he spoke'.

Commenting on this odd little scene Tony Tanner suggests that Jane Austen would not have been surprised by any of Sigmund Freud's formulations on the workings of the subconscious mind. Tanner sees the episode, that is, as a projection into symbolic outward action of an intense inner desire to cut through intolerable restraints —but if one is going to talk in these terms it seems to me that one must push the Freudian interpretation to its logical conclusion in the sexual sphere, with scissors as an obvious though of course unconscious phallic symbol.

Obviously in the time at my disposal I can't deal in any detail with all of Jane Austen's novels from this point of view, to my great regret. *Pride and Prejudice*, of course, marks a great advance in Jane Austen's artistic subtlety and control. As in so many of her novels the central theme is the painful progress from illusion to reality, from a false estimate of the outside world and of the inner self to the truth about both. This theme, whose end is indeed reality, is, however, again conducted by means which are by no means strictly realistic. There is an almost balletic element in the structure of the novel. Elizabeth and Darcy first see each other at the Merryton Assembly Rooms: they dance uneasily together at the Netherfield ball—and the exchanges between them thereafter have something of the formal movements of an eighteenth century dance, as they approach, circle cautiously round each other, abruptly retreat, to hover round each other again, until after further approaches and withdrawals they unite as partners.

There are, too, patterned groupings of characters whose formal nature is now concealed by the greater subtlety of Jane Austen's art. As in *Sense and Sensibility* there are two sisters and a double plot. In each a heroine is fascinated by a villain whose secret has to be divulged—the initial attraction Elizabeth feels for Wickham should not be overlooked: even when he has dropped her she excuses him on the grounds of his poverty, and is still 'convinced that, whether married or single, (Wickham) must always be the model of the amiable and pleasing'.

There are also times when the characters dispose themselves as if they were taking part in a Morality Play devoted to the subject of Pride. Take, for example, the scene when the Bennets are all together at the Merryton Assembly Rooms. All (with the exception of Jane) display various aspects of Pride. Mrs Bennet is snobbishly proud of Jane's imagined prospects; Mary shows off at the piano; Mr Collins boasts of his patronage by Lady Catherine de Bourgh: Mr Bennet indulges his usual ironic detachment in enjoying what he calls his family's 'performance' (a form of inverted Pride); and Elizabeth indulges *her* pride in her sense of superiority over her family (though eventually she will have to realise that she, too, is a Bennet).

And there is at least one scene which is close to allegory: the episode in which Elizabeth's aunt and uncle, the Gardiners, take her to Darcy's estate, in the mistaken belief that its owner is away from home. The Gardiners are in effect Elizabeth's guides and mentors, in bringing her down to the world of decent, unpretentious values (Mr

Gardiner, after all, lives 'by trade, and within sight of his own warehouse').

The progress of the little party is a symbolic enactment of Elizabeth's own inner feelings and self-discoveries. The Gardiners 'guide' her through the grounds and into the house. Mrs Gardiner (who has always been suspicious of Wickham) then guides Elizabeth to two miniatures, one of Wickham, the other of Darcy. Next, she guides her to two full-size portraits of the same pair. Then out in the grounds again, they are confronted by Darcy himself. It is almost as if Mrs Gardiner had conjured him out of thin air. Elizabeth finds Darcy's manner 'strikingly altered'—but the change is largely the result of a change in herself. The real action in the scene is symbolic and psychological, and the plot itself has become a kind of allegory for the inner drama. Elizabeth and Darcy are both aware of it and the awareness is registered in the look which passes between them. And at this level of poetic intensity the novel has in a sense already ended when on the lawn at Pemberley the eyes of Elizabeth and Darcy meet in an as yet unconscious acknowledgement of the fact.

Time dictates that I must say even less about *Persuasion*, Jane Austen's last novel. It differs from all the others in one important respect—the central crisis has already taken place when it begins. This naturally involves changes in technique of a freer, more impressionistic kind—the use, for example, of flash-backs. There is never any doubt as to the existence of the love between Anne and Captain Wentworth, and the real theme of the novel is the healing powers of those eight years that have elapsed since the parting of the lovers, in the spirit of Shakespeare's 'ripeness is all', or T. S. Eliot's 'redeem the time'—and there are many phrases in the novel like 'time will tell' and 'as the event decides'. There are alarms and excursions on the way to fulfilment, but there is always a sense that nature is working in its slow, inexorable way and will eventually prevail.

All this means that *Persuasion* is—naturally—more poetic and allegorical. To take just a few of the more obvious instances. The sea and the people who belong to it are evoked both by way of contrast to the arid way of life represented by Sir Walter Eliot, Bart., and as a symbolic opening out to wider emotional horizons. The whole business of Mrs Smith and her crony Nurse Rooke, who open a window on a very different world behind the facades of polite society, is almost Dickensian in its allegorical atmosphere and its whiff of melodrama. And what of Louisa Musgrave's famous fall on the Cobb at Lyme

Regis? Does she jump because she wants to test out Captain Went-worth's willingness to catch her? And does he fail to do so because he doesn't really want to, because subconsciously it is another woman he wants to gather in his arms? The novel is full of such intriguing questions.

What I must do now, though, is concentrate on the two novels which, it seems to me, most comprehensively illustrate what I have called the non-realist elements in Jane Austen's fiction. In a course of lectures on masterpieces of world literature which Vladimir Nabokov gave in America in the late 1950s he chose as his seven examples *Bleak House*, *Dr. Jekyll and Mr. Hyde*, *Madame Bovary*, *Swann's Way*, *Metamorphosis*, *Ulysses* . . . and, at the top of this curious list, *Mansfield Park*. Speaking of it he said: 'there is no such thing as real life for an author of genius: he must create it himself and then create the consequences'—and went on to assert that 'the characterisation of *Mansfield Park* can be fully enjoyed only when we adopt its conven-tions, its rules, its enchanting make-believe'—and he compared it to a fairy tale.

The fairy-tale analogy may strike one as startling: but I think one could at any rate see *Mansfield Park* as a blend of fable, Morality Play—yes, and fairy-tale in which Sir Thomas Bertram is the Father with a capital F, in whose absence anarchy threatens to take over, but who at last returns, descending like a *deus ex machina* to restore Order and Harmony; this would make Tom Bertram the Prodigal Son who is also a Lord of Misrule; the Crawfords the Tempters, bringing with them a whiff of brimstone; the dreadful Mrs Norris would pass muster as a combination of Witch and Wicked Stepmother. And little Fanny Price? A Cinderella who eventually finds her prince? An ugly duckling who turns into a swan? Patience on a Monument? Virtue, with a capital V, reminiscent perhaps of the heroine of Milton's *Comus*? This is being fanciful, but all these ingredients are, so to speak, held in suspension beneath the surface of the novel, and at times the language bears witness to them—as, for example, when Edmund Bertram, cured of his infatuation for Mary Crawford, says: 'the charm is broken. My eyes are opened'.

It would be ridiculous, of course, to ignore the fact that *Mansfield Park* belongs to a specific historical and social context, written as it was between 1811 and 1813 at a time when a period of stability was already giving way to one of rapid and far-reaching change, when a new spirit was already abroad, greedy and speculative (it is significant that at the Grant's house they play a game called *Speculation*—not unlike the modern *Monopoly* in spirit—and morally significant too that Henry Crawford is by far the best player, and Fanny the worst). It would also be ridiculous to overlook the fact that Jane Austen as the daughter of a Tory parson was personally attached to the old traditional rural values, represented by Sir Thomas and his Mansfield Park.

In many respects, in fact, *Mansfield Park* is a 'condition of England' novel. Not, though, of the kind represented by, say, Mrs Gaskell's *North and South* or Disraeli's *Sybil*. Closer, rather, to E. M. Forster's *Howard's End* in its poetic, semi-impressionist methods, and open therefore, to timeless symbolic and psychological interpretations over and above the contemporary social and historical significances. As far as these significances are concerned, Jane Austen uses groups of characters to denote opposing sets of values in somewhat the same way as Forster does with the Wilcoxes and the Schlegels. Jane Austen, though, really has three opposing sets: those embodied in Mansfield Park; those belonging to Fanny's Portsmouth family—not actively wicked but their home an 'abode of noise, disorder and impropriety'; and those of the smart London world represented by Henry and Mary Crawford. Mansfield Park can absorb Portsmouth (it has already taken Fanny and in due course will accept her brother William and her sister Susan). But there is no possibility of a Forsterian 'connection' between Mansfield Park and the Crawfords, other than one which would destroy Mansfield Park, and all it stands for.

The central—or pivotal—part is played by Fanny. On the face of it she is a most unlikely Jane Austen heroine, for she is small, sickly, physically weak, inactive, and excessively shy and retiring. She is also, which is perhaps more difficult to swallow, *never wrong*. Yet she is the one heroine who has her creator's unqualified approval and who is completely vindicated at the end.

To understand and appreciate Fanny one must take account of her unique relationship to Mansfield Park. She is the daughter Sir Thomas *ought* to have had—his actual ones, Maria and Julia, don't fit the bill at all, and Fanny is the only one in the family who believes utterly and unshakeably in the values of stability and tranquillity represented by Mansfield Park, a place where, Fanny reflects after her visit to Portsmouth, there were 'no sounds of contention, no raised voice, no abrupt bursts, no tread of violence'. But Sir Thomas himself is a flawed God: for example he eventually admits to Fanny that he has brought up his children with too great a concern for money and status;

that he was wrong in admitting the odious Mrs Norris into his household, and that he was wrong in trying to persuade Fanny to accept Henry Crawford's proposal for purely worldly reasons. And at the end he realises that Fanny's natural place *is* as a daughter, married to Edmund and close to the heart of Mansfield Park.

Now as Sir Thomas is not an altogether satisfactory embodiment of the values for which Mansfield Park stands, it is Fanny who is their true guardian, and doubly so when Sir Thomas has to go away on some unspecified business in the Caribbean, and Mansfield Park is threatened from within and without. No wonder that Fanny is so often ill: the strain imposed by such a 'guardianship' might have taxed a far stronger constitution. To the disruptive influences that now invade Mansfield Park, Fanny opposes her steadfast sense of what it *should* be—and her *stillness*. It is not, however, a passive stillness, and Jane Austen subtly conveys the fact by setting against it the amiable but utterly inert passivity of Lady Bertram, who is quite incapable of representing her husband in his absence.

The great threat to the stability of Mansfield Park is that posed by the arrival in the neighbourhood of the Crawfords. They represent an irruption of London values into the rural ethos. The fact that they don't understand the country is nicely caught in the incident of Mary Crawford's harp (fitting symbol for a siren!)—she is puzzled, you will remember, why no cart is available to transport the harp, unaware that it is harvest time. The Crawford's real home is Regency London—the London of glamour, excitement, amusements, smart wit, casual relationships, false appearances, manners as a substitute for morals, and above all, restlessness—everything, in fact, that Mansfield Park is *not*.

Jane Austen was much too good a novelist to render this opposition between London and Mansfield Park in simple black-and-white terms. The Crawfords are also genuinely charming and attractive. It is easy to see why they have struck many readers as the only source of vitality in the novel. It is to Mary, for example, that all the wit belongs. It is she who says of a clergyman who is rumoured to be having an affair: 'As Dr M. is a clergyman, their attachment, however immoral, has a decorous air'. Or this: 'I am sorry for the Beaches' loss of their little girl, especially as it is the one so much like me.' And again: 'Mrs Hall . . . was brought to bed yesterday of a dead child, some weeks before expected, owing to a fright. I suppose she happened unawares to look at her husband'.

It is noticeable, though, that Mary's cracks contain a core of heartlessness, and a touch of the *risqué*. Those I have quoted, by the way, first appeared in Jane Austen's own letters, but in another later letter she wrote: 'wisdom is better than wit', and increasingly in her fiction she assigned wit to characters with whom she was not fully in sympathy.

So the essential heartlessness of Mary Crawford's wit is symptomatic of what London has made her. The good qualities which she and her brother potentially possess have been corrupted by London. They infect the Bertram children with their own London values—and Tom, Maria, and Julia are in fact all corrupted when *they* go to London themselves.

And Fanny is the only one aware of the spreading infection. She is the still centre in the midst of impending chaos. It is she who sees 'the influence of London very much at war with all respectable attachments', and that the charming Henry Crawford 'could do nothing without a mixture of evil'.

All these issues are encapsulated in two of the most remarkable symbolic sequences in English fiction. The first of them is the excursion to near-by Sotherton, the home of the feeble Mr Rushworth, to whom Maria is engaged, for purely worldly reasons—though Henry has already begun to flirt with both Maria and her sister Julia, and both are very much aware of it.

Mr Rushworth takes them on a tour of the great, gloomy mansion. He shows them the chapel, though explaining that it is no longer used for family prayers with all the servants assembled. 'Every generation has its improvements!', Mary quips, 'with a smile to Edmund' —though Fanny regrets the passing of the old custom. As Maria and Mr Rushworth stand at the altar, further jests follow about their forthcoming marriage, accompanied by 'a look of meaning' from Henry to Maria. It is appropriately in the chapel, too, that Mary learns that Edmund is going to be ordained, and determines to laugh him out of so humble a profession. As Fanny senses, in fact, there is an air of levity about the company's behaviour in the chapel which is not consonant with the place—or the calling Edmund has chosen.

They all return to the main part of the mansion, where, however, they experience a feeling of claustrophobic confinement. Mrs Rushworth and Mrs Norris begin to organise a tour of the grounds. The young people ignore them—and 'meeting with an outward door, *temptingly* open . . . as by one *impulse, one wish for air and liberty,* walked out' (my italics).

I stress those words and phrases because they are so clearly indicative of a sudden and dangerous moral relaxation.

Outside Henry reveals himself as an avid 'improver' (in the eighteenth century sense of altering the design of grounds in order to make them more 'picturesque'). It is another symptom of his inner restlessness, his desire for change for change's sake—and it aptly echoes his sister's comment on 'improvements' in the chapel. He advises Mr Rushworth, for example, to chop down a whole avenue of ancient trees. Only Fanny recoils from the idea—she has brought her sense of guardianship with her.

It is a hot, oppressive day, and the whole party is aimless and fretful. The air is taut, too, with subterranean feelings—the growing infatuation between Edmund and Mary; the flirtation between Maria and Henry; and Julia's pent-up jealousy because of it. Now they split up. Mrs Rushworth and Mrs Norris remain apart, and Julia, furious and resentful because Henry is with Maria, stays with them. The others move on through the gardens, and the whole episode becomes increasingly symbolic, taking on those mysterious, timeless effects we might find in a film by Antonini or Fellini, and creating a strange, hypnotic atmosphere in which actions, words and phrases increasingly take on special emphases and vibrations.

First, Henry and Maria, Edmund, Mary and Fanny pass through the formal gardens and lawns—the area, that is, still tamed and civilised—and then into the 'wilderness'—in other words the less civilised part. Here Mary sets out to undermine Edmund's intention of entering the Church—with Fanny, like a small voice of conscience, speaking in his other ear. There is a bantering argument between Mary and Edmund about the 'distance' they have travelled (again in more senses than one) with Mary insisting that since they left 'the great path' (the *straight* path?) they have pursued 'a very serpentine course'—and as the choice of words suggests the verbal fencing between the two is in effect a kind of furtive preliminary love-making.

When Fanny complains of tiredness the three of them sit down on a rustic seat. But soon Mary, characteristically, is saying: 'I must move . . . resting fatigues me'—and she persuades Edmund, with no difficulty at all, to take her into the wood, holding on to his arm. Fanny is left alone, a still centre of awareness and resistance. Her tiredness is the result of the drain on her spiritual resources.

Then after a while Maria, Henry and Mr Rushworth join her. But they, too, are uneasy and restless. Maria notices an iron gate on the other side of a ha-ha leading out of the wilderness and into the parkland—the uncultivated, least civilised part of the estate. She expresses a wish to explore it. But the iron gate, the image of the restrictions imposed by the requirements of civilized life, turns out to be locked. Mr Rushworth explains that the key is back at the house. He, after all, as Maria's fiancé, *is* the rightful owner of the key: it is for him to unlock the gate. The hidden sexual implications here, it seems to me, are inescapable, and it is perhaps relevant to recall that in medieval paintings a locked garden was often used as a symbol of virginity.

So Mr Rushworth hurries back to the house to get the key. The conversation between Henry and Maria that follows is full of *doubles entendres* no less inescapable. Henry tells Maria: 'I shall never see Sotherton again with so much pleasure as I do now. Another summer will hardly improve it to me'. He is hinting, of course, at Maria's coming marriage to Mr Rushworth. So, too, when a moment later he speaks of 'the smiling scene' now in fact before her eyes, equating it with her 'fair prospects', her reply is: 'Do you mean literally or figuratively? Literally, I conclude. Yes, the sun shines and the park looks very cheerful'. And then she adds: 'but unluckily that iron gate that ha-ha give me a feeling of restraint and hardship'. She walks towards the gate—'with expression', we are told—and Henry follows her. 'I think,' he says 'you might, with a little difficulty pass round the edge of the gate here, with my assistance; I think it might be done if you really wished to be more at large, and could allow yourself to think it not prohibited.' Surely I am not being fanciful in detecting sexual undertones in these exchanges? Although Mr Rushworth arrives a few minutes later with his key, the episode undoubtedly prefigures Maria's eventual adultery with Henry.

In the meantime Edmund and Mary are still wandering in the wood. No wonder that when Mr Rushworth says to Fanny that he thinks it a great pity the Crawfords had come into their lives 'a small sigh escaped Fanny' (she is, after all, in love with Edmund). It is she who now sends Mr Rushworth in pursuit of Maria and Henry. She is left alone again, aloof from the antics of the others, a small figure of moral tenacity while they dangerously roam. When they all assemble again there is once more a taut, uneasy feeling in the air, an irritable disharmony, as if some irreparable damage had already been done, and the seeds of future disaster sown.

The expedition to Sotherton is a prelude to the other semi-allegorical set-piece in the novel—and one of the most remarkable sequences in English fiction. The inane Mr Yates—another intruder from the world outside Mansfield Park—suggests that they act a play. The others, with the exception of Fanny, fall avidly upon the idea. But what might in other circumstances have been a simple bit of fun— *if* nerves and emotions had not already been over-excited by the Sotherton expedition—soon degenerates into something closer to Carnival, with all its implications of the snapping of controls. In fact the very idea of performing a play at Mansfield Park in its present situation, and in the absence of Sir Thomas, is a dangerous one, as Fanny, of course, instinctively recognises. The folly, moreover, is compounded by the choice of play. It is *Lover's Vows*, an adaptation by Mrs Inchbald of Kotzebue's *Das Kind der Liebe*—'the Child of Love'—which had been first performed in London in 1798. The plot, very briefly is this: the chambermaid Agatha is seduced and abandoned by the suggestively named Baron Wildheim. Unknown to him she bears him a son, Frederick, who years later learns the secret of his birth, and to help his starving mother tries to rob the Baron, without knowing who he is. After he is arrested Frederick realises the truth, and reveals his identity. Helped by the pastor, Anhalt, he persuades the Baron to marry his mother. The Baron also allows his coquettish daughter Amelia to marry Anhalt instead of the foppish Count Cassel whom he had chosen for her.

Obviously enough, a play featuring seduction, illegitimacy and the forward behaviour of Amelia towards Anhalt was quite unsuitable, under any circumstances, for young people in the moral climate of the times, and utterly alien to what Mansfield Park stands for. Fanny, again, is aware of the fact, and deeply disturbed by it. All the participants, indeed, realise that Sir Thomas would have disapproved. But that, for them, is part of the wild attraction, and it is Tom, who as the eldest son ought to be the most responsible, who directs the play. As for Edmund, he too is uneasy, but by now he is too bewitched by Mary to make any effective protest—and needless to say she and her brother are the most enthusiastic of all.

When it comes to casting, the usual in-fighting and manoeuvring takes place, but intensified by all the secret passions and jealousies involved. In the end the parts are assigned exactly as the Crawfords have intended: Agatha, the mother, is to be played by Maria, and Frederick the son by Henry—which means they will be playing some highly emotional scenes together. Mary secures the part of the flirtatious Amelia, and persuades Edmund, after some initial reluctance on his part to play opposite her as Anhalt. Mr Yates takes the part of the Baron, and Mr Rushworth that of the foppish Count Cassel. Julia, who had hoped to get the part of Agatha, so that *she* could play opposite Henry, isn't cast at all, and flounces off with the words 'Do not be afraid of *my* wanting a character'—which has a double meaning in view of the fact that the others are busy losing *their* characters.

The most inappropriate piece of casting is that of Edmund, who is going to be a clergyman, *as* a clergyman, and the object of Amelia's —that is Mary's—attentions. It is almost as if he is renouncing his vocation. But Fanny alone is aware of these implications. In effect the play-acting at Mansfield Park is really an extended metaphor to illustrate the further rapid deterioration that had set in since the visit to Sotherton, and to mark the climax of irresponsible licence in Sir Thomas's absence. 'They were relieved from all restraint', Jane Austen significantly comments, when once 'the inclination to act was awakened'—and in the process the values represented by Mansfield Park are almost destroyed.

The theatricals are also a symbolic means of exploring the whole issue of role-playing, as it affects both the individual and society, both in Jane Austen's day and increasingly as time went by. As Fanny knows, if Mansfield Park is to stand, one must be true to oneself. This concept is reiterated time and time again. Maria and Julia, we are told, are deficient in 'self-knowledge', and Julia lacks 'a knowledge of her own heart'; Fanny refers to Dr Grant's 'knowledge of himself'; Edmund feels a disparity 'between his theatrical and his real part'; and later he reminds Mary of 'the most valuable knowledge we could any of us acquire—the knowledge of ourselves'—and so on. And Fanny, when the others first try to make her join in the theatricals cries: 'I could not act anything if you were to give me the world! No, indeed, I cannot act.' For she is the one who, by remaining true to herself also remains true to Mansfield Park.

Jane Austen is not being puritanical about the theatricals as such (as we know she thoroughly enjoyed them herself). She is showing that *in the context of Mansfield Park* the play-acting involves the danger of the inner self being swamped by the false one . . .

or, if you like, of the Ego being fractured by the irruptions of the Id.

It is significant that the only ones completely immune to uneasiness are the Crawfords. 'If I had the power of recalling any one week of my existence,' Mary says later, 'it would be . . . that acting week'; and Henry—who is 'considerably the best actor of all'—echoes her sentiments when he says: 'We were all alive . . . I was never happier.' But then, the Crawfords only feel alive in a world of continuous movement, variety, and outward appearances, and when they are playing one role after another in it. They have no real inner lives, or at any rate only the withered remnants of them.

The theatricals, then represent the most serious threat to Mansfield Park and the values it embodies. It comes very close to success. For Fanny is suddenly called upon to take Mrs Grant's part (in one of the minor roles) when that lady falls ill. The pressure upon her is so great that she nearly succumbs. It is as if her moral strength has been so severely sapped that it is no longer sufficient by itself to sustain Mansfield Park. But then Sir Thomas unexpectedly returns and order is restored.

Nabokov's use of the fairy-tale analogy could perhaps be applied with even greater plausibility to *Emma* (1816). The heroine, it is true, is a 'poor little rich girl' rather than a Cinderella or Ugly Duckling. But there are also elements in her of a Princess immured in an enchanted Castle, weaving fantasies about the outside world, or even of a Sleeping Beauty waiting for a Prince Charming to release her from the spell. It would be ridiculous, of course, to push the analogy too far. Hartfield, after all, is a very cosy castle, and Emma is 'the fair mistress of the mansion'. But the idea of a claustrophobic enclosure is certainly there—and it is appropriate to this idea that Emma is the only heroine of Jane Austen's never to have been to school, never to have spent a night away from home, never to have seen the sea, never to have been to Bath or London (only sixteen miles away) and all these factors denote both the unusual degree of concentration *on* the heroine (we see nearly everything through her eyes) and emphasise her extreme isolation, cultural, moral, and above all emotional.

One might go so far as to say, moreover, that the castle has its ogre. That is an unjustifiably harsh word to apply to the amiable Mr Woodhouse. But it would be wrong to see him a harmless old fuddy-duddy. Like so many hypochondriacs he is self-centred to the point of solipsism: as Jane Austen points out he is 'never able to suppose that other people could feel differently from himself', and his kindnesses are in essence those which are conducive to his own comfort. He treats all marriages as funerals ('poor Miss Taylor' is his refrain after Emma's governess and only close confidante has left to marry Mr Weston). This is funny and ironic, but it also means that he is hardly the kind of father to help his daughter towards maturity. It is, in fact, largely because of her father that Emma is encapsulated in her little world of Hartfield, with no real emotional life of her own. Her only life-line to the real world, in fact, is Mr Knightley.

It is Jane Austen's purpose, of course, to lead Emma into that real world—and to him. But again the methods she employs are often different from those of straightforward realism. There is, for one thing the whole strange business of Emma's adoption of Harriet. Emma turns her into what is in effect a combination of pretty puppet, stalking-horse and romantic heroine by proxy. As Harriet can offer no challenge or opposition, Emma is free to use her as a vehicle for her fantasising. Just as Catherine in *Northanger Abbey* invents a Gothic Abbey that doesn't exist, so Emma invents a Harriet who doesn't exist—in order to dodge the pain of escaping from a prison which she cannot recognise as such and which she thinks she loves. So she can declare of Harriet without the least shred of evidence that 'there can scarcely be any doubt that her father is a gentleman—and a gentleman of fortune'. This idea of Harriet as in effect a creation of Emma's is borne out by many words and phrases: for example we read 'Emma spoke for her'; when Harriet timidly ventures an observation of her own Emma peremptorily cries 'Leave it to me!'; and when Mr Elton admires a drawing Emma has made of Harriet he says 'skilful has been the hand', almost as if Emma, Pygmalion-like, were moulding Harriet out of clay. Mr Elton, it is true, is trying to play Emma's game by wooing her *via* Harriet. Needless to say she can't see it. When he makes his intentions clear, her conclusion is 'He must be drunk!' He has refused to conform to Emma's scenario. She is momentarily jolted out of herself, but she is soon at it again. Her second scenario for Harriet, you will remember, has Frank Churchill as romantic hero (after she has tried out the idea for herself). First, though, she has done some inventing of Frank too. 'My idea of him . . .' she is saying before she has even set eyes on him, and Jane Austen comments sardonically on 'those views on the young man, of which her own imagination had already given her such instinctive knowledge'. Into the bargain Emma invents Jane Fairfax, the young woman who has come to Highbury to stay with her aunt Miss Bates. When Emma hears that Jane has refused an invitation to visit her close friend, married to a Mr Dixon, 'an ingenious and animating suspicion' enters her mind, and she proceeds to quiz Miss Bates 'with the insidious design of further discovery'. Jane Austen's choice of that word 'insidious' is important: it points to a morbid, almost prurient element now entering Emma's behaviour, the result of her ingrown state of mind, her almost pathological condition.

It is evident in particular in her sly questioning of Frank about Jane and her relationship with Mr Dixon, and her decidedly nasty comments on his replies. When, for instance, Frank tells her that when they were all at Weymouth (Frank included—the real import of *his* presence never crosses her mind) it was Jane not her friend, Mr Dixon's future wife, whom he called upon to play the piano, Emma suggest that Jane 'must have felt the improper and dangerous distinction', and—almost smacking her lips, one feels—adds that if Jane 'continued to play whenever she was asked by Mr Dixon, *one may guess what one chooses*'. And when a piano arrives for Jane, Emma of course jumps to the conclusion that it is a present from Mr Dixon, and not from Frank.

In Frank, though, Emma has met her match. In his determination to conceal his secret engagement to Jane, he connives at Emma's fantasies—over and above the call of duty, one might say, for a very strange relationship develops between him and Emma: he allows himself to become a sort of puppet or mimic, but, unlike poor Harriet, a conscious one. 'Why do you smile?' Emma asks him when they are discussing the piano. 'I smile because you smile', is Frank's reply. And again, speaking to Emma: 'I told you that your suspicions would guide mine'—while at the Coles' party 'smiles of intelligence' pass between Emma and Frank, though Emma is quite blind to those between Frank and Jane.

The steps in Emma's gradual awakening from the spell that holds her are embodied, above all, in three quasi-allegorical set-pieces. The first of these is the ball at the Crown, where Jane Austen again makes use of the imagery of the dance. It is Frank who first leads Emma on to the floor—but 'She was more disturbed by Mr Knightley's not dancing, than by anything else'. She looks at him and thinks how distinguished he is in comparison with those around him. It is the first time the idea of Mr Knightley as a physically attractive male has entered her head. When he asks her to dance with him and she complies with the curious words 'We are not really so much brother and sister as to make it at all improper', his heartfelt response, you may recall, is 'Brother and sister! No indeed!'. So Frank has led her onto the dance floor, but it is Mr Knightley who leads her off. It is a symbolic portent of the time when Emma will have broken out of the cocoon of her fantasy life, and can start having a real one of her own.

The second episode is the strawberry picnic at Donnington, Mr Knightley's home. Emma has often seen it before, but now she does so with different eyes, hurrying from place to place 'eager to refresh and correct her memory with more particular observation, more exact understanding'. Like Elizabeth's visit to Pemberton in *Pride and Prejudice*, it is a symbolic drawing closer together of the two people concerned.

It is, though, the expedition to Box Hill which forms the outstanding semi-allegorical sequence: one which is both dream-like and powerfully evocative—and which if it were being filmed, would demand all kinds of strange camera angles, tilts and swoops.

It is a hot, sultry day—as it was at Sotherton in *Mansfield Park*. As there, too, 'there was a languor, a want of spirits, a want of union which could not be got over. They separated too much into parties, there was a principle of separation'. It is a picture of a society torn within itself and of a disruption in the human psyche itself, brought about by mutual hostilities and suspicions, and above all by the secret tensions between Frank and Jane (their marriage plans at this point are in disarray), and by those gathering painfully in Emma's soul.

Then comes the strangest passage of all, increasingly dream-like, as if the heat of the day is shimmering on the edges of another dimension. Emma sits apart from the others, as if distancing herself from the hard, factual world. But with Frank in attendance, like a sorcerer's apprentice one might say, for he plays an oddly subservient role, though one with a dash of malice in it. 'You are comfortable', Emma tells him, 'because you are under command'. 'Your command?' 'Yes'. In her fretful, desultory mood Emma now uses him as a go-between with the other group. 'Ladies and gentlemen', he says as he approaches them 'I am ordered by Miss Woodhouse (who, wherever she is, presides) to know what you are thinking of'. Then, a little later: 'I am ordered by Miss Woodhouse to say . . . she demands from each of you either one thing very clever . . . or two things moderately clever—or three things very dull indeed, and she engages to laugh heartily at them all'. 'That will just do for me, you know', kind garrulous Miss Bates says referring to the third alternative—and there follows Emma's famous snub.

To snub Miss Bates, in the psychological context of the novel, is no light matter. She fulfils an important function in it and in Emma's awakening. She is, pre-eminently, the character who sees the world exactly as it is—'What is before me, I see,' are her own words. In her rambling monologues about all kinds of domestic details, family and local gossip, lie buried the simple truths about the world which Emma must enter, when once she has broken the spell of Hartfield.

After this, as if some intangible crisis has taken place, the behaviour of Emma and Frank becomes even more peculiar. Frank still pretends to be obedient to her every whim, and at the same time, with her compliance, to be conducting an oblique flirtation with her. 'Will you choose a wife for me?', he asks, 'I am sure I should like anybody fixed on by you . . . Adopt her, educate her . . .' 'And make her like myself?' Emma interrupts. 'Very well', she agrees a little later, 'I undertake the commission. You shall have a charming wife'. She is thinking of Harriet, but acting as her stand-in, just as Frank is making her *his* stand-in for Jane. The blending of emotions and motives, however, produces a blurred effect, almost as if the two characters had run into each other, and it is accompanied by a taut, rather ugly atmosphere. 'The young man's spirits', we are told, 'now rose to a pitch almost unpleasant'. Frantic, almost feverish, in his anxieties about Jane, his exchanges with Emma lose their playfulness: his sallies take on a tinge of mockery as if he is beginning to hate his companion because she is *not* Jane. He can no longer take any pleasure from pretending to be a partner in her game of make-believe. Neither can Emma. Her own inner desperation is mounting, and she is gnawed by guilt over her behaviour to Miss Bates. When Mr Knightley hears of it and administers a sharp rebuke, Emma is deeply moved, and 'felt the tears running down her cheeks'. She still has a long way to go, but those tears are a sign that the carapace that has enclosed her is beginning to melt.

When I was thinking of a title for this talk I nearly chose '*Surrealist elements in Jane Austen's Fiction*'. I decided, though, that it would be too grotesque to place Jane Austen in the company of Chirico or Salvador Dali! When I think, though, of that sequence at Box Hill or of the expedition to Sotherton or the theatricals in *Mansfield Park*, I'm not so sure. There *are* elements in her work that call for some such term. It may be that all so-called realistic novels of any profundity contain them, and perhaps we need a new word, like supra-realistic. In any case, my title has enabled me to draw attention to aspects of Jane Austen's fiction that interest me—while of course leaving out all kinds of other important ones. I hope that at the least I have been able to demonstrate that there *are* elements that stretch out beyond the bounds of purely conventional realism.

Wedmore Memorial Lecture

IVOR GURNEY AND THE 'POETIC SENSIBILITY'

P. J. KAVANAGH FRSL

Read 19 October 1989
C. H. Sisson, FRSL, in the Chair

THIS PUTS FORWARD the tendentious thesis that poets complain too much, and praise too little. But its real purpose is to advertise the poetry of Ivory Gurney. One way of doing so is to begin by having a look at the reasons why, about 1919, when he became a genuinely original poet, he immediately lost his publisher. He never found one again, although on the whole, he wrote, better and better. Such an investigation may throw some light on what we expect from poetry in different epochs, tell us something about the nature of the readership of poetry, and therefore about ourselves; it may even suggest something about the nature of poetry itself. Indeed, a professional teacher of English Literature, Professor John Lucas, after the publication of Gurney's *Collected Poems* in 1982, said that if Gurney were to be incorporated into the canon, as in Lucas's view he had to be, we would have to re-think our whole idea of what poetry is.

Gurney was born in 1890 and died in 1937; his most fruitful period was in and around 1922. Volumes of his wartime verse were published in 1917 and 1919; it was mellifluous (although already, in 1919, there were some complaints about the colloquialisms), fairly conventional in sentiment, and it made no great demands on the embarrassment-threshold of the reader. As he matured as an artist he found a more direct access to some nub of simplicity in himself and, in his own phrase, 'free of useless fashions', there came a great outpouring of poetry which, perhaps because of its simplicity, although there were other reasons, made his publishers take fright.

What was wrong, to contemporary taste in 1919, at least as interpreted by poetry-editors, in this simplicity? What were the other reasons? And why has it taken so long, if he is any good, for Gurney to obtain a hearing?

In one word, and that is too few, it is because his directness was embarrassing, it was out of tune with his time, and it has remained out of tune, and embarrassing, for different reasons, to succeeding changes of taste.

For example, he uses queer mixtures of everyday language and the grandiloquent—but cannot be safely labelled 'modern'.

He sometimes uses 'Shakespearian' made-up grammar, elisions, and so on—but this is neither recognisable pastiche nor to be dismissed or forgiven as 'old-fashioned'.

He does not conform to any easily recognisable tone, or presumed readership—yet he addresses the reader confidently, intimately, as if sure of being understood, and this is always bound to disconcert somebody.

He goes on, with equal unselfconsciousness, about the noble Romans, the lads in the trenches, England's greatness, his pantheon of acknowledged masters—William Byrd, Bach, Ben Jonson, and the rest—yet he mixes this with the small details of English middle-class or lower-middle-class life—the pleasures of tea-time, small incidents of local history. You cannot quite place him, you never know where he is going to take you.

Maybe, and it is perhaps what John Lucas meant, we are now at last able to take on board the varieties of subject and tone Gurney managed to get into his verse, sometimes into the same poem. Modern realism, a fidelity to the flow of the mind, even modern magic realism, may have made us more elastic in this respect.

But before we begin to congratulate ourselves, let us look at this matter of being embarrassed by the over-direct, by the absence of a saving irony. We pride ourselves on being unshockable but despite this George Steiner has called ours 'an age of embarrassment'; embarrassment, that is, at any mention of all the old absolutes, beloved of Gurney—art, love, country, transcendence. Steiner has said that we can now get away with any corner of the mouth remark, and he comes up with a marvellous phrase—'the corner of the mouth has replaced the human tongue.'

This is understandable. In our age we have received more shocks to our notion of ourselves than can be easily sustained. Scepticism, irony, are a natural defence. We have become streetwise. If this is so, if we are indeed in 'an age of embarrassment' then we have need of a poet who puts himself consciously above such a limitation, who abjures it because he thinks it unworthy of art, which is meant to be the truthful expression of the whole of life, not just selected parts of it. We need him because he may help us examine the causes of our embarrassment and recognise them for what they are, which is a form of fear.

Gurney is such a poet. But when, after his work had disappeared for thirty years, Edmund Blunden rescued and printed a selection of it in 1954, the event passed more or less without notice. Gurney's obvious clumsiness, so often in his best poems intentional and a source of their extraordinary music, his daring Elizabethan way with syntax and coinages and word-order, above all his subject-matter, which is often his native Gloucestershire, made it easy to shunt him into a siding, dismiss him as an incompetent hick, a queer Georgian, a 'local' poet. But Gurney's Gloucestershire was not a limitation, although every poet needs the particular as a starting-point; it was a backdrop for landscapes and skyscapes and sweeps of history and for the emotions aroused by experience of these; in fact his are love poems to the world, often a pained and baffled love. Even his poems about the First World War are a sort of love poetry to the world, and perhaps this is why they went for so long unnoticed, because they did not complain enough and were therefore puzzling. They made no general statements about war itself but concentrated on the clink of mess-tins, the rise of dawn above the trenches of France. Also, in these poems, there was always the surprise of his diction, to puzzle one, or to put one off. He can conclude a war poem—'So silence fell, Aubers front slept,/And the sentries an unsentimental silence kept./ True, the size of the rum ration was still a shocker/But at last over Aubers the majesty of dawn's veil swept.' So, there are all sorts of ways of avoiding Gurney, who himself avoided so little. Now his collected poems have been published we have less excuse.

Reviewing these on their publication in 1982 Donald Davie concludes: 'This Gurney was a prodigious poet: beside his achievement

Wilfred Owen's and Edward Thomas's seem slender at best. And
Eliot? And Pound?' asks Davie. 'Why yes, take them too in, say,
1925, and Gurney has out-distanced them—in the range of first-hand
experience he could wrestle into verse, and even in the range of past
masters in English whom he could coerce and emulate so as to digest
their experience. The strain of the achievement was intolerable, and it
broke him. Just why or how it's impossible to say: though it seems he
set his face against irony, and irony, which we have over-valued for so
long, is often—as we have learned to our cost—self-defensive.'

So Davie, in 1982, brings us to Steiner in 1989—'the corner of the
mouth has replaced the human tongue'. We can argue with Davie's
comparisons and claims for Gurney. It is unnecessary to use one poet
to knock down another, but Davie is publicly asserting high status for
a poet still barely known; certainly his range is not known. What is
true is that Gurney always uses his tongue, never the corner of his
mouth, and this has a curious effect; when we are confronted by
certain of his poems, above all by his poems collected together,
although of course they are not all equally successful, and once we
have got over our initial shock and even embarrassment at their lack of
evasiveness, and linguistic quirkiness, we feel in the presence, not
only of poems, but of poetry itself. What is true of one man's
experience, so fearlessly stated, and however clumsily, we see to be
true for us all, we become for a moment part of a brotherhood and
sisterhood, and this is surely because he is always just to his experience, just to life.

To explain what I mean by 'just to life', which is a daunting topic,
and before returning to Gurney, I would like to begin with a poem by
someone else, the American, Richard Wilbur, called 'Cottage Street',
1953, about a meeting he had with the young Sylvia Plath:

Cottage Street, 1953

Framed in her phoenix fire-screen, Edna Ward
Bends to the tray of Canton, pouring tea
For frightened Mrs. Plath; then, turning toward
The pale, slumped daughter, and my wife, and me.

Asks if we would prefer it weak or strong
Will we have milk or lemon, she enquires?
The visit seems already strained and long.
Each in his turn, we tell her our desires.

It is my office to exemplify
The published poet in his happiness,
Thus cheering Sylvia, who has wished to die;
But half-ashamed, and impotent to bless.

I am a stupid life-guard who has found,
Swept to his shallows by the tide, a girl
Who, far from shore, has been immensely drowned,
And stares through water now with eyes of pearl.

How large is her refusal; and how slight
The genteel chat whereby we recommend
Life, of a summer afternoon, despite
The brewing dusk which hints that it may end.

And Edna Ward shall die in fifteen years,
After her eight-and-eighty summers of
Such grace and courage as permit no tears,
The thin hand reaching out, the last word *love*.

Outliving Sylvia who, condemend to live,
Shall study for a decade, as she must,
To state at last her brilliant negative
In poems free and helpless and unjust.

There will be those who disagree with those words about the work of Sylvia Plath, but I quote them only for my purpose, which is a discription of the practise of Gurney. Let us focus on the last word of that good poem—the word 'unjust'. We can agree, I think, that poetry has almost wholly lost the public function with which it began. It no longer celebrates the history of the tribe, the deeds and deaths of chieftains, our relationship with God or the Gods. It has therefore inevitably become to some degree, and in a variety of ways, personal. Exceptions can be found, and I am talking specifically about English poetry, nevertheless, in the main I believe that this emphasis on private personality, however disguised, the case can be recognised as generally. The question arises therefore, in a poetry that is likely to be personal and brief, whether in some cases it is therefore almost certain to be 'unjust', and whether poets ought to be on their guard against this.

To explain in that word further, 'unjust'—unjust to life, which I take it is what Wilbur meant—let us imagine in an obvious way the possible inception of many such poems.

A poet, or at least someone who attempts to write poems, is looking out of a window at dawn on an autumn morning. He may be in bed, a soft rain may be hissing outside. He is warm, and alert, and suddenly he feels at the back of his mind a sense of some great joy, glimpsed, almost understood, that might, with luck, herald that small spasm of excitement that Seamus Heaney has called 'the only excuse for the conception of a poem'. But a poem about the arrival of joy while lying in bed looking out of a window, even in the always unlikely event of it being a good poem, would not only be difficult to write, it would have to leave out too much. That unexpected joy which came like an access of grace—as it might have been described in another age—would surely have arrived in part because of a release from some strain, and if that particular discomfort could also be brought to consciousness it would have to be described but would spoil the poem, would probably *become* the poem, and the joy be left out altogether, although the joy was the point. Also, the poet would know that part of the emotion he felt at that tranquil moment would relate to some lucky childhood memory of feeling safe and snug in bed, would therefore be infantile. None the worse for that perhaps, but infantile nevertheless; even 'unmanly', in the worst sense, and this is an accusation Gurney levelled against himself, calling his fancies 'girlish', as we shall see. Indeed, the popular stereotype of the poet is often considered ineffectual and effeminate in that way. So, all sorts of considerations like this would enter the poet's mind and some between him and his brief visitation. (Gurney, incidentally, called his poetry, 'the child of joy'.) No wonder poets can become mentally paralysed. As Philip Larkin remarked, the poems a poet wants to write are not always the ones that get written. In this way the danger of being unjust to certain kinds of experience is always there.

Should the poet be of a religious cast of mind—and it is difficult to think of a poet who is not—he would recognise something religious in the joy, all-inclusive, akin to the peace that can sometimes be achieved by trust in a merciful creator; the great joy that can be found in release of praise for creation, praise of life, which, with love of our neighbour, is surely the most inclusive human activity, and therefore the most just. Love of our neighbour? The poet knows he has received this particular insight most acutely because he is alone, no one else is yet awake in the house; we must hurry, he thinks, or human voices wake us and we drown. He could scribble the poem quickly, but successful scribbles are more rare than is sometimes supposed. By the time he comes to work on the poem all sorts of demands and distractions will

have crowded in on him and the poem will therefore most probably
contain an element of regret about this, a note of elegy for time past
and lost; it might even for this reason contain anger, and bitterness. It
would therefore be unjust to the original experience, the initial gift or
impulse. It would be unjust because it had had to adjust to a different
reality—some might say to richer and more complex reality, but the
poet would not necessarily agree. It is therefore possible that in a sense
all contemporary poetry tends towards the 'unjust' in this way, if the
poet is not careful, and—this is the point—it is the hallmark of Gurney
that his readers feel that this is precisely the care he took. He remained
faithful to his original impulse, which is why, if you like, he can be
embarrassing.

Not many poets succeed in being true in this way, and sometimes,
ruefully, they admit it. Robert Lowell ends an Afterword to one of his
books of poems with the words: 'In truth I seem mostly to have felt the
joys of living; in remembering, in recording, thanks to the gift of the
Muse, it is the pain.' Gurney suffered more pain than a man should,
and said so, but he is not like Lowell, is not so passively subservient to
the Muse. He got down the joy also, which is perhaps what Davie
admired, 'in the range of first hand experience he could wrestle into
verse'. 'Wrestle' is a good word, for there is much that is consciously
manful in Gurney's verbal struggle, though, as we soon shall see, he
chided himself for having 'a girl's fancies', as though he could grow
impatient with the innocence of his own impressions. But there is
surely something odd about an attitude to verse, confessed to by
Lowell, which feels compelled by inspiration to leave out of description 'the joys of living'. The picture of life it presents must to an extent
be 'unjust'. No wonder Marianne Moore begins a poem, about poetry,
'I, too, dislike it.' But, she goes on: 'Reading it, however, with a
perfect contempt for it, one discovers in it, after all, a place for the
genuine.'

It has this place, I would suggest—and this is another thorny
subject—because of poetic form. A good poem is a defiance of time, it
creates its own time, an internal musical pulse, which also must
contain a regret for external time, which it can never quite overcome.
But the attempt to overcome it must be made, which is why Richard
Wilbur constructs his resonant anecdote about Sylvia Plath with such
evident care for tune and pulse; it is also why he suggests in the poem
that although he is there as a poet to recommend life, and cannot help
feeling fatuous, he does recommend it, 'despite/The brewing dusk

which hints that it may end.' Honesty compels him to add that. Leaving aside the matter of form—which Gurney for the most part solved by rhyme and by trusting, rightly, his ear, this twin problem, the duty to celebrate, and the equally great, though somewhat easier, duty to report the pains and disappointments of experience, is at the heart of Gurney, because he faced it with courage. It would even be possible to risk saying that the difficulty of these twin responsibilities drove him mad, for the near-impossibility of the reconciliation of the two duties, praise and blame, is indeed maddening. It is much easier to settle for mere description of disappointment. He tackled the problem directly, in two versions of the same poem, which is itself unusual for him; when dissatisfied with a poem he usually wrote an entirely different one on the same subject. The second version has only recently come to light in manuscript.

Before we examine these two attempts it might be worth having a brief look at Gurney's history, and the history of his manuscripts.

He was born in 1890 in Gloucester, the son of a tailor; went to the Royal College of Music and became a composer who could set poems to music in a way, according to his biographer and others, which bore the stamp of genius. He also had signs of mental imbalance. In 1915 he joined the Gloucestershire Regiment as a Private, which he remained, and deprived of a piano he began to write poems. These were published with some success. After the War he could not settle; between 1919 and 1922 he wrote a mass of poetry and music, and as far as poetry is concerned it was some of his best. In 1922 he was certified insane and was confined to an asylum for the next fifteen years until his death in 1937. In the asylum he continued to write, often brilliantly, until 1926. Then, if his surviving manuscripts are anything to go by, he stopped, after he had finished by writing a series of classical lyrics, almost Vergilian in tone, exquisite in their music, from which the personal is wholly excluded. The year before that, 1925, must have been a bad one for him because he went back to old poems and changed them, nearly always for the worse, for he included his new confusions and his indignation at his confinement. In the early selection of his work Edmund Blunden printed some of these and they had the effect of putting people off, retarding recognition of his clearer work.

In the early 1970s a box of notebooks came to light which contained much new material and hand-written versions of poems already printed which made it possible to clear up the many typing errors that had crept into the two editions of Gurney so far published. Thus an enlarged and more accurate collected edition of his poems was enabled to be published of which I was the editor.

However, in 1986 a further handwritten notebook came to light. Why it was not found among the original boxes of papers is not clear. Perhaps because Gurney had entitled this notebook, 'Best Poems', it caught somebody's eye and had, so to speak, fallen off the back of the lorry. It is however a late notebook, very possibly belonging to that bad period, 1925, when Gurney tended to make poems rambling and confused which in their original versions had been clear. Nevertheless it does contain versions of poems for which, in 1982, no manuscript could be found, and it would have been useful to see these before the *Collected Poems* went to print. It also contains a second version, or at least a hitherto unknown manuscript version, of a poem printed in the collected edition, and it is these two poems that we look at now. Neither of them is of his best, though both are interesting, as Gurney usually is. For those unused to his elisions, a little explanation may be helpful, after we have looked at each poem. Gurney admired what he called 'the football rush' of Chapman, and even practiced readers sometimes have an initial difficulty when first confronted by the fooball rush of Gurney. There will also be an attempt to explain what the poems mean, which should never be done, or only when trying to support a tentative thesis, of the infantile and passive and 'feminine' nature of the poetic sensibility, which is Gurney's subject in both poems, and which he regards as more of a hindrance than a help. The printed version, called 'Song'.

Song   (MS 64.7)

I had a girl's fancies
At the pools—
And azure at chances
In the rut holes
Minded me of Maisemore
And Gloucester men
Beside me made sure
All faithfulness again.

The man's desiring
Of great making
Was denied; and breaking

To the heart much caring—
Only the light thoughts
Of the poet's range
Stayed in that war's plights.
Only soul did not change.

So to the admiration
Of the rough high virtues
Of common marching
Soldiers; and textures
Of russet noblenesses
My mind was turned
But where are such verses
That in my heart burned?

I shall gloss that, for my own sake as much as for anbody else's. He begins at once with what I have dared to call, following his lead, the 'feminine' nature of the poet, which is of course not necessarily a bad thing, though here he finds it disabling. He is talking of the pools of water in shell-craters and the ruts made by wheels of gun-carriages. He admires, he feels in too predictable and 'poetical' a fashion, like an out-of-place Georgian, the 'azure at chances', which are the occasional reflections of blue sky which these puddles contain. These remind him of home, of Maisemore, a little village by the Severn, and the cheerful presence beside him of men from his own county makes him equally predictably want to celebrate them too. He feels himself—and it is not to stretch the figure too far—looking out in safety, as it were, from a bedroom window, at the beauty of men and of the world, feeling the usual poetic emotions—and in such circumstances these are not enough, too much is being left out. The second verse says so. Gurney was dedicated, to the point of obsession, to art, to the act of creation, to extracting art from himself. After the war he starved himself and went without sleep in order to devote himself wholly to art, in words and music. Yet, 'The man's desiring/Of great making/Was denied . . .' Only the lighter thoughts, the obvious beauties of sky-reflection and the simple heroism of his comrades came to his pen, he found his soul insufficiently changed by his experiences, too much of external reality was being omitted, and therefore too much of internal reality also. He hadn't done it, set it down, expressed it fully enough—'But where are such verses/That in my heart burned?' He feels that the poem he manages to set down is, to use a colloquialism, 'wet'.

Partly his difficulty, as we can see, comes from his inability to be unjust. He cannot *help* admiring the sky in shell-holes, and the russet nobleness of his companions, and refuses to edit this out. The 'word 'russet' is noteworthy. Gurney is not a guileful or obviously deft poet (though early on he was) but he remained more consciously skilful than at first appears. That word puts us in mind, appropriately, of Cromwell's 'plain, russet-coated captain', and also, of course, of apples. There are still apple-orchards round Maisemore.

His subject is the struggle within his temperament with the matter of poetry itself, and as we readers work to understand him we are drawn into the struggle, or, as Davie would prefer, the wrestle; we become involved in the wrestling-match, which is a part of Gurney's technique. He forces the reader to be on unusually intimate terms with him.

Now the second version, if it is the second version, though the darkening, and the increased confusion, strongly suggests that it may be.

> *Song*   ('Best Poems' MS)
>
> I had a girl's fancies
> At the pools;
> Azure at many chances;
> Limber rut holes—
> Or shells at the dumps.
> And a poet's welcome
> To see the night lamps
> Of France, so like home.
>
> But the girl in me went out
> In Gommecourt trenches.
> Minnewerfers—wooers stout
> The only wenches.
> And the poet died wholly
> East of Vermand—
> Before wires, and bullet tears.
> Lying puzzled on wet land.
>
> But the soldier kept both
> Saw Rouen's blue river,

Tawny rock, high of faith;
And after Arras weather.
No blighty for a poet
No such luck for him
Ypres dawns hurt his heart,
Flanders dusk dim.

We have lost Maisemore and now have the night-lamps of France instead; he is trying to get nearer the immediate experience (though both poems were written after the war). Minnewerfers were a kind of German rocket-grenade, much feared. Here the girlish poet-part of his nature which over-admired the night-lamps, dies wholly, 'lying puzzled on wet land'. It is hard to think of any line, of equivalent simplicity, more appropriate to the experience of a trench soldier in the First World War. The word 'puzzled' is perfect—what are we all doing here? asks the soldier, what are we doing to each other?

The last stanza is a problem and it seems fair to risk the following interpretation: the inadequate poetic part of the girlishly poetic Gurney is dead, whereas the ordinary practical soldier is able to keep both parts alive, the poetic part of his nature and the practical part, therefore his responses remain intact. Gurney had relied too 'girlishly', unrealistically, on the first part, and it had been put out by real experience, like a light. I am as certain as I can be that he does not refer to himself as 'the soldier'; he never, without humble qualification, gave himself that title.

But for him the problem of being a poet will somehow not go away. 'No blighty for a poet/No such luck for him'. A 'blighty', of course, was a wound sufficiently severe for you to be sent home; it was also leave, a holiday. Thus Gurney in the third stanza seems to be saying the opposite of what he said in the second, to be now affirming that he is still a poet, still bound without relief to suffer and observe. For this reason it is a more muddled and muddling poem than the one published, but is a second attempt to analyse, even to shrug off, that part of being a poet, and therefore of being extraordinary, that in his view prevented a poet from reacting appropriately and therefore healthily to ordinary experience. There is a kind of democratic heroism in it.

But the point of Gurney, or one of the points, is that he used this disappointment in expression to be part of the expression itself; as a means, consciously deployed or not, of involving the reader. Not long before he was taken to the asylum in 1922, possibly in the same year, he wrote an eight-line poem in which he seems overcome by his presumed failure to capture the transient

Moments

I think the loathed minutes one by one
That tear and then go past are little worth
Save nearer to the blindness to the sun
They bring me, and the farewell to all earth

Save to that six-foot length I must lie in
Sodden with mud, and not to grieve again
Because high autumn goes beyond my pen
And snow lies inexprest in the deep lane.

But that snow *is* expressed, at least for this reader perhaps because of the adjective 'deep', and certainly because of what has led up to it; we see the snow, almost because he has told us we cannot. He has recruited our imaginations to his assistance.

But none of this would be worth saying if Gurney's wrestle with what he considered the 'over-poetic' in himself, together with (if it does not amount to the same thing) his inability to be unjust to experience, the way he could not help the celebration of the apparently irrelevant and transitory—the flowers by the roadside they marched along, the candle-shadows on the low roof of the dug-out, these noted as facts, not as emblems of something else—if these had not enabled him to write some of the most real (it seems the only word) war- and nature-poems in the language. So real, in fact, and so used are we to commentary on the game rather than the game itself, that they can seem to escape the bounds of what we consider to be literature, and it has taken us seventy years to realise that they are within it, or if not there is something wrong with the boundaries. They are so near to the fact of the matter that Gurney barely trusted them himself; but now, almost without hope of publication, perhaps because of that, he indulged himself, indulged his so-called girlish fancies and put into his poems whatever he thought they required. Thus he remained true to the dawn-responses of his nature, which could admire the sky reflected in pools of destruction, appreciate the warm hiss of rain as he looked out from his trench, or looked out of a window in Gloucestershire, on Crickley Hill. He has a poem called 'Looking Out', which contains the regret, the elegaic quality to which poetry tends, but he is also careful to admit the comfort, and that is part of his distinctiveness, his incapacity to be unjust.

Looking Out

First for the hanging curtain—
Next for the breeze—
That hangs in the light wind waving,
Comfort in these

Familiar things, gone out
From the preoccupied
And too-busy present-mind
To some deep inside.

But in old days
How were present the sighted
Everyday things the mind
Infinitely delighted.

And all the rewards, O where
Are they misted, withered,
All into time's waste heap
Taken-up, gathered.

By 'rewards' he surely meant the rewards of his wonder at the world, which he felt he deserved. Indeed, 'Rewards of Wonder' was the title of his third collection of poems, rejected by his publisher, which was more or less the end of his public career as a poet while he lived.

We have seen how he despaired of getting the whole of his experience into verse, how he felt this was because of 'a girl's fancies', insufficiently profound and inclusive, but he remained an original poet, precisely because he failed to stifle these fancies, refused to become sophisticated, sceptical, ironic, to use the corner of his mouth. Failed? His letters, funny, practical, sharp in his criticism of his fellow-poets, show us the 'failure' was intentional. It is strange that we have to turn to his letters to save ourselves from the suspicion that he was unconsciously naive in his poems, it shows how unused we have become to being in the presence of such directness of feeling. His decision to stay faithful to the core of simplicity in himself could be described as a refusal to grow up; it was also a refusal to be unjust to life, which was so unjust to him. By reason of this refusal he can sometimes get the most astonishingly diverse things into the same poem, and they hang together. He asks, 'Where are the verses/That in my heart burned?' In the end, he wrote them, or some of them.

Of all poets, perhaps, Gurney in his confinement had the right to regret the passing of joy, who had begun with so much of it. But in a poem written late in his writing-life he can still wring an unforgettable music of this, in a poem that syntactically almost collapses inwards on itself, but not quite, it recovers, and the recovery is part of the excitement. In it he is musing, near a favourite time of the year for him, All Saints' Day, which he calls after the French fashion 'Toussaints', on his past as a music student, his nervous breakdown and how he told his fellow-soldiers about it, and they misunderstood. He remembers the churches of his beloved Gloucester, which he has not been allowed to see for years; the church of St Michael, of St Nicholas, and the two churches dedicated to Mary. He manages humour, about the way his fellow-soldiers regarded musicians, and about their pidgin French. He even manages to get in a plug for himself as 'a War Poet', it was a new category, and he wants to stake his claim for membership. (At the head of one his manuscript war poems he had written 'To knock out Robert Graves'. At the bottom he had written 'Unsuccessful'.) He does belong to that company now, officially. His name is on the tablet dedicated to 'the War Poets' that was recently unveiled in the Poets' Corner of Westminster Abbey.

That may have pleased his shade. Perhaps it pleases the shades he addresses in this poem, written in the asylum when he had been long forgotten by the world. It is a poem about being thus forgotten, but it uses so many registers, shifts of tone and thought and music, includes so much, that somehow it contrives to create a balance, manages to remain just. There was little enough joy in his life by this time, but, in the phrase of Robert Lowell's with which we began, 'thanks to the gift of the Muse', it is not only the pain that he remembers.

It Is Near Toussaints

It is near Toussaints, the living and dead will say:
'Have they ended it? What has happened to Gurney?'
And along the leaf-strewed roads of France many brown
    shades
Will go, recalling singing, and a comrade for whom also
    they
Had hoped well. His honour them had happier made.
Curse all that hates good. When I spoke of my breaking

(Not understood) in London, they imagined of the taking
Vengeance, and seeing things were different in future.
(A musician was a cheap, honourable and nice creature.)
Kept sympathetic silence; heard their packs creaking
And burst into song—Hilaire Belloc was all our master.
On the night of all the dead, they will remember me,
Pray Michael, Nicholas, Maries lost in Novembery
River-mist in the old City of our dear love, and batter
At doors about the farms crying 'Our war poet is lost,
Madame—no bon!'—and cry his two names, warningly,
    sombrely.

Joseph Bard Memorial Lecture

CONRAD ALONE

JOHN HALPERIN FRSL

Read 19 May 1988
Gavin Young, FRSL, in the Chair

'Very few sailors can swim. . . . They are fatalists.'
V. S. Pritchett

'SHE IS no bother at all,' Joseph Conrad wrote of his wife Jessie, in 1896, to Edward Garnett. 'As a matter of fact, I like to have her with me.' They were on their honeymoon.

Conrad was thirty-eight and had been alone most of his life. As a child he had been shuffled from one place to another due to the anti-czarist activities of his father and their consequences, including the early death of both of his parents. He went to sea at seventeen, retired from it at thirty-five, and tried the profession of writing. He set foot in England for the first time at twenty, and began to learn English properly in his early twenties. He had, as Edith Wharton was to remark, worshipped the English language all his life like a lover, but had never romped with it in the nursery. He was uncomfortable in company with other people—perhaps in part because being with others required him to speak to them, and this he disliked to do. 'I have never been very well acquainted with the art of conversation,' he admitted years later in his autobiographical memoir *A Personal Record* (written 1908; published 1912). 'My young days, the days when one's habits and character are formed, have been rather familiar with long silences.' In English fiction, at any rate, Conrad was to be silent for many years, largely because of the circumstances of his life. He did not attempt any fiction in English until he was twenty-eight, he did not begin to *write* anything in English until he was thirty-one, he did not *publish* anything in English until he was thirty-seven.

Conrad's 'young days' were as solitary as it was possible for them to be. He was born in what was then Poland and is now the Ukraine on 3 December 1857 and christened Jozef Teodor Konrad Nalecz Korzeniowski. When Conrad was three his father Apollo Korzeniowski was arrested for carrying on clandestine political warfare against Poland's Russian rulers; one of the future novelist's first recorded deeds was the sending of pastries baked by his grandmother to his father in prison. In 1862 Apollo, his wife Evelina, and their young son, an only child, were sent into Siberian exile. It was in Siberia, in 1865, that Conrad's mother died. He was seven. Suffering from tuberculosis and a semi-invalid, Apollo Korzeniowski wrote despairingly to a friend in Warsaw that his boy 'is of course neglected . . . Poor child: he does not know what a contemporary playmate is.' Young Conrad was given some schooling in the Siberian exile he shared with his father. He could read from the age of five, but apparently he never saw a child's book. Of his first son Borys, Joseph Conrad wrote to a friend in 1899: 'I can't confess to any reverential feeling for childhood. I've heard people, more or less sentimental, *talk* about it but I question whether it is not a rather artificial attitude.' For Conrad, childhood was something that others, even his own son, only *allegedly* had: he possessed no intuitive understanding of what the term meant.

In 1869 Apollo Korzeniowski died, and Conrad's nominal childhood abruptly ended. He was eleven. He was passed now from a friend of his father's to his maternal grandmother and on to some of her aristocratic friends and finally to a maternal uncle, Tadeusz Brobowski, who was to become the guardian of his adolescent years. Conrad was sent to a series of Polish schools, found that his favourite subject was geography, and began smoking cigars. At fourteen he made two declarations: he disliked the Christian religion, he said—its doctrines, its ceremonies, its festivals; and he wished to become a sailor. Besides Polish and Russian he knew German: he thought he might begin his career as a sailor by escaping to Austria or Germany, for he could not see himself living under the rulers who had murdered his parents. He read travel books by the score, and in one by his compatriot Jan Kubary he found the following passage: 'What today

happens on land can evoke nothing but contempt, and seclusion at
sea is a hundredfold more pleasant than life among men.' Death at sea,
where there is no politics, was preferred by Kubary to life on land
because at least, in the former instance, 'you lie in a free grave.' One of
the few friends of Conrad's youth recalled years later that the boy had
a habit of spinning fantastic yarns whose action always took place at
sea. Conrad saw the sea for the first time when he was fifteen, from the
Lido in Venice. He travelled for several months in Switzerland, which
was bursting with Russian political exiles and, years later, would
become the setting of *Under Western Eyes* (1911). In October 1874,
two months shy of his seventeenth birthday, equipped only with
clothes and books and fluent in French, Conrad left the home of his
Polish uncle and set off for Marseilles and the career at sea he had been
dreaming about. He was, of course, by himself, as he had been more
or less for years. What was his natural environment? Where were his
family and friends? What, indeed, was his nationality, and what was
his native language? He seemed to have none of the usual human
attachments and possessions. Physically, psychologically, spiritually,
he was alone.

During the next four years, from 1874 to 1878, Conrad lived in
Marseilles. A large and rich and lively place, a center of trade and
smuggling, a meeting place between East and West, Marseilles
fascinated him with its swarming temptations and opportunities.

In July 1876, as a steward in the French Merchant Marine, Conrad
sailed in the barque *Saint Antoine*. The first mate was a Corsican
named Dominic Cervoni, later the model for Nostromo. The *Saint
Antoine* called first at Martinique and then made for South America,
with stops in Colombia and Venezuela. Conrad got off the ship at La
Guaira in Venezuela and acquired the small material he needed years
later to reconstruct the country of Costaguana in *Nostromo* (1904).
Everyone agrees that the South American setting of what is perhaps
his greatest novel is as vivid and unforgettable as the setting of any
work of fiction; the fact is that the eighteen-year-old Conrad, nearly
three decades before *Nostromo* was published, spent only a few days in
'Costaguana' and never strayed far from the coast.

There is disagreement about the cargo of the *Saint Antoine*. The
ship may well have been involved in smuggling guns to the conservative rebels in Colombia; in later life, at any rate, Conrad enjoyed
describing his career as a gunrunning smuggler. After stops in the
Virgin Islands and Haiti, the *Saint Antoine* returned to Marseilles in

February 1877, and Conrad, now nineteen, had completed his first voyage as a seaman.

A year later he supposedly tried to kill himself. There are various accounts of the run-up to this affair, the more romantic ones involving, again, the smuggling of arms—this time to Spain for the supporters of Don Carlos, the Bourbon Pretender to the throne. This is the subject of Conrad's late novel *The Arrow of Gold* (1919). A doomed imbroglio with a girl named Rita adds spice to the story in some of its versions. The facts are that Conrad invested what little money he had in the cargoes of ships sending contraband to Spain, lost every franc, and felt oppressed by this financial catastrophe. He got himself seriously into debt. There were desperate schemes to recoup. He thought of running off to join an American squadron at Villefranche, but this came to nothing. He tried his luck at Monte Carlo with some money he borrowed, and lost every penny of it. Worst of all, it appeared that, as a Russian subject, he might have to give up the French Merchant Marine and serve instead in the *Russian* army. 'Rita' may well have been an invention; it is certainly more romantic to say that you are in despair over a woman than to say that you are in debt. In any case, on a pleasant evening in Marseilles, Conrad invited his chief creditor to tea, and just before the man's arrival shot himself in a fleshy part of his upper body. No organ was touched by this famous bullet, and the addresses of his physician and his closest relatives were conveniently left in the clear view of his visitor so that the help he would need, both medical and financial, could be instantly summoned. Conrad's uncle paid his debts; no more was heard of 'Rita' until many years later, when this pathetic episode was transformed by Conrad's memoirs into an interesting attempt to take his life after his first disappointment in love, which occasioned a duel. Conrad never fought a duel. The scars on his body were the result of his deliberately bungled suicide attempt, and the 'duel' was invented to explain the scars. What is important here is what *actually* happened. Conrad's was the anguished act of a hapless youth who needed help and knew no other way to ask for it.

The year 1878 was an important one for Conrad, and for English literature. In the spring of this year he sailed as an ordinary seaman from Marseilles to the Sea of Azov and then to Lowestoft. He saw England for the first time in June 1878, aged twenty. He joined the British Merchant Marine that same summer and took the first of his many voyages as a British sailor. In the 1870s over half the ships afloat around the world were British, men were in considerable demand to serve in them, and no special permits were required for enlistees, foreign or domestic. The no-questions-asked policy made things quite simple for Conrad—much simpler than if he had tried enlisting in the 1880s, by which time steam was considered more economical than wind, and jobs on sailing ships were getting scarce. In later years Conrad was fond of saying that he always intended to be a British seaman, but the process by which he became one could better be described as serendipitous than inevitable.

Indeed, it could hardly be described as anything else, since Conrad, at the time he first reached England, intended to return to France and join the French navy, at least in part to escape Russian conscription. He had no money and he could not, in 1878, speak a word of English. Despite his later version of events, he became a British sailor in the first instance because he needed the work, the money, and the anonymity, and he happened to find himself in a place where all three were to be had for the asking. And so he sailed for two months in the latter half of this year as an ordinary seaman on the *Skimmer of the Sea* between Lowestoft and Newcastle. He got another British ship, this time the *Duke of Sutherland*, and on it, again as an ordinary seaman, he sailed to Australia and back in 1879. In 1880 he served in the *Europa* between London and several Mediterranean ports. It was during these years (1878–80) that he began to learn English.

This is not the place to sketch a contemporary history of the British Merchant Marine, but something must be said of the sort of life an ordinary seaman was likely to lead on ships in those days. Crews of such vessels, as Zdzislaw Najder has described them, were for the most part city riff-raff, castaways, vagabonds, and waifs. An ordinary seaman lived in constant danger of disablement or death while doing what was in effect routine work; there was no disability insurance. The men who sailed before the mast might develop physical courage, or absolute indifference to human life, or perhaps a stoical combination of the two. Certainly courage and cowardice, as well as savage indifference, are depicted in Conrad's tales of the sea. Despite what people today might think, few chose the sailing profession during the latter decades of the nineteenth century for the sake of adventure, or love of the sea, or to 'gather material'; usually the alternatives such men faced were worse. Sailors with some education enlisted in the Royal Navy; aboard merchant vessels most of the men were there, quite simply, because they needed the miserable remuneration and knew no safer way to earn it; or because they wished to drop out of sight, and this was a good way to do it. Conrad, who feared both debt and Russia, felt relatively secure in the hold of a British ship. In no sense could it have been an easy life. But, as Conrad said of the English flag, it was 'destined for . . . many years to be the only roof over my head.' In fact he lived at sea or nowhere.

Now, at twenty-two, Conrad took another of those decisions which in retrospect came to seem momentous. The son of exiles, and of an age to be conscripted, theoretically he was now obliged to do military service in Russia or to be shot as a deserter should the Russians lay their hands on him. He would be safe from Mother Russia only by climbing out of the ranks of ordinary seamen and becoming an officer. Officers in the British Merchant Marine traditionally were exempt from conscription. And so he applied to sit the examination for second mate. One of the requirements was passable English, and this spurred Conrad on to improve his latest adopted language. Another was a minimum of forty-eight months at sea, a requirement which in fact he was nowhere near able to satisfy. But Russia was calling. Conrad quickly got his friends in the French service to cook up some documents which were then submitted to the British service; he was risking indictment for perjury had the fraud been discovered. But it wasn't. In June 1880 he was allowed to take, and passed, the examination for the second mate's certificate. Probably he never forgot that the first step he took up the ladder of the British Merchant Marine was founded on deceit and forgery, though of course he never spoke of it in later years.

He obtained his first job as an officer on the *Loch Etive*, in which he sailed not as second but as third mate to Australia and back in 1880–81. This was a ship of the iron clipper class, engaged mainly in the wool trade. Conrad's pay was three pounds and ten shillings per month. The next examination he would have to take if he wished to advance in his profession was that for first mate, and the reading he did to prepare himself for this step helped secure his grasp of English. Still, he had not, except in the course of duty or some other necessity such as an examination, *written* a word of English, and he was twenty-three. Can there ever have been, in the history of literature, a more incredible thing? Here was a man destined to become indisputably one of the greatest writers the world has known, who, in his twenties, was not able to *compose* in the language in which his greatness was to be achieved.

In September 1881, at 4 pounds a month, Conrad signed on as second mate of the *Palestine*, a ship in which he was destined to serve—more or less, as we shall see—until March 1883. The *Palestine* would take him to the Far East for the first time—its initial destination was Bangkok—and it would become the model for the *Judea* in one of Conrad's earliest literary successes, 'Youth' (1902). In the story and in fact the vessel's captain was named Beard and its first mate Mahon; often enough Conrad could not be bothered to invent names.

The *Palestine* embarked for Bangkok in November 1881, lost a mast, and started to sink before it got out of the Channel. It limped back to Falmouth, where repairs took over eight months. In September 1882 it finally sailed for Bangkok, encountering its final disaster much nearer the shore line than the *Judea*'s end as described in 'Youth.'

The crew of the *Palestine* was taken to Singapore, where in March 1883 a court of enquiry cleared all officials and crew of responsibility for what was in effect the ship's spontaneous combustion. Coal and grain were the most dangerous cargoes, being so flammable, and the *Palestine* had been carrying coal. Conrad had to wait in Singapore for a ship. While languishing there he became sufficiently acquainted with the harbour district to use it later as the setting of several of his tales, including one of his best: *The Shadow Line*.

In 1883, for the first time, the number of steamships exceeded the number of sailing ships. The demand for sailing officers was dropping sharply. Conrad, feeling that he was too old a hand to start learning the principles of navigation by steam—he never did learn them, but rather retired from the sea around the time sailing ships became virtually obsolete as long-haul freighters—Conrad decided to study for his first mate's examination; this might make him more marketable as an officer. In the autumn of 1883 he sailed aboard the *Riversdale* as second mate with a crew composed largely of Scandinavians, to South Africa and India, places he made little use of in his fiction. The return journey from India to England (June to October 1884) was immortalized thirteen years later by his first tale of the sea, for this ship was called the *Narcissus*.

In November 1884 Conrad sat, and failed, his examination for first mate, an event which goes unmentioned in *A Personal Record*. His failure was largely the result of a poor performance in the section called Day's Work, which consisted of questions about navigation based on entries in the logbook, the ship's position, speed, and so forth. He went to a crammer and tried again. This time, in December 1884, he passed. In the same month he turned twenty-seven. As the number of officers' jobs continued to decline, Conrad began to work for the master's examination. But the market for ship's officers remained depressed, with opportunities at all ranks becoming scarcer as more and more shippers turned to steam.

After a long search, in the spring of 1885 Conrad found a ship. This was the *Tilkhurst*, and he signed on as second mate—he could not get a first officer's position—at 5 pounds a month. The *Tilkhurst* unloaded cargo in Singapore and Calcutta, and from these ports Conrad dispatched to a Polish friend living in England some of his earliest extant letters. Interestingly, he wrote in English rather than in Polish. The letters are full of current British politics: Conrad, it appears, had become an ardent Tory. Where his father had been a noted liberal, the son took a different line—inspired in part, no doubt, by the contempt he felt for the only sort of men he had known well since he went to sea at seventeen, the urban and port riff-raff he was to describe so scathingly in several of his tales. For he was a fastidious and ambitious man, just now starting to feel in earnest that he inhabited the wrong world. The son of upper-middle-class parents, he was beginning to feel *déclassé*.

Conflicts with port rabble and a decline in the discipline of work on the part of sailors must have been among Conrad's reasons, and those of many of his fellow merchant officers, for an unfavourable attitude not only towards ordinary seaman but also what they represented potentially and symbolically: incipient trade unions and socialist agitation.

In the spring of 1886 the *Tilkhurst* returned to England, and during that summer—indeed, within twenty-two days of one another—two important events overtook Conrad. In July he failed the master's examination. Again he performed poorly in Day's Work, and this time also in mathematics. In August a much more important event occurred: Conrad officially became British.

His naturalization papers were approved. He had long since discovered that the first and third of his five Polish names were the easiest for Englishmen to pronounce, and so Józef Teodor Konrad Nalecz Korzeniowski became Joseph Conrad. Now no longer one of the czar's subjects living illegally abroad, he was transformed, by the stroke of a pen, into one of Queen Victoria's subjects—indeed, one of her most loyal ones. In connection with this changeover, Conrad had to pay a visit to the Russian embassy at Chesham House, Belgrave Square—called Chesham Square in *The Secret Agent* (1907), which describes the embassy carefully.

Encouraged now to persevere, he applied himself with greater urgency to his studies for the master's examination, and passed it in November. He had become, at the age of thirty, a British captain, though one without a ship. But at least he occupied, finally, a recognized position. Certainly he had few if any influential friends. Of the four acquaintances who testified on his naturalization application to his good character, three were fellow mariners, none had known him for more than five years, and two had known him for two years or less.

One other event of the year 1886 must be mentioned. It was during this year that he tried his hand for the first time at a piece of fiction-writing. The weekly *Tit-Bits*, a popular digest of the sort so unmercifully satirized by Gissing in *New Grub Street*, sponsored a short story competition, and for it Conrad wrote a tale called 'The Black Mate'—probably an early draft of what would become, in 1897, *The Nigger of the 'Narcissus'*. The story did not win the competition, and in all likelihood was destroyed in manuscript.

'The Black Mate' is significant in other ways. It further helps dispose of the myth, now generally discredited anyway, that when Conrad began to write *Almayer's Folly* he hesitated between English and French. *Almayer* could have been written only in English. 'English was for me neither a matter of choice nor adoption,' Conrad declared some years later in *A Personal Record*. 'The merest idea of choice had never entered my head . . . if I had not written in English I would not have written at all.' Also important is the testimony offered by composition of 'The Black Mate' to Conrad's general discontent with the seaman's profession (despite his recent promotion), his frustration with his life as it was, and his need for cultural contacts and activities which might help him to overcome the single most potent fact of the first thirty years of his life: his isolation. Finally, we should note that the story he submitted to *Tit-Bits* was a tale of life at sea. It is not surprising that the world he wished to leave was the world he knew best.

Conrad's maritime appointments always seemed to lag behind his qualifications. Since he had passed his first officer's examination he had served only as a second mate. Now that he had his captain's certificate, he finally found a position as first mate. The salary was 7 pounds a month, and the ship was the *Highland Forest*, to which he was attached throughout the first half of 1887. The *Highland Forest* took him from Amsterdam to Java; the captain, McWhir, reappears as master of the *Nan-Shan* in the brilliant novella *Typhoon* (1903). Conrad did encounter, while in Singapore, a steamer called the *Nan-Shan*, which was used for transporting hundreds of Chinese, as in *Typhoon*. In the course of the trip to Java, he was injured by a falling spar. He spent some time, during July 1887, recuperating in the European Hospital in Singapore—described in *Lord Jim* (1900), whose hero, also hit by a falling spar, is treated for his injury in the same hospital.

During the short trip (four days) from Semarang to Singapore for treatment, Conrad met, aboard the SS *Celestial*, Frederick Havelock Brooksbank, son-in-law of the well-known merchant and sailor William Lingard, the original of Tom Lingard in *Almayer's Folly*, *An Outcast of the Islands* (1896), and *The Rescue* (1920). Conrad never actually *met* William Lingard, but he was regaled, during the four-day journey to Singapore, with tales about him from two of his nephews, who by chance were travelling with Brooksbank in the *Celestial*. Conrad became friendly with Brooksbank, who introduced him to the master of a small steamer called the *Vidar*. Destined to play a crucial role in Conrad's life, the *Vidar* made regular voyages between Singapore and Borneo, where one of Lingard's nephews had been living for some years as a trading agent.

And so in August, from Singapore, Conrad embarked on what would turn out to be one of his most significant journeys. It was as first officer of the *Vidar*, which between August 1887 and January 1888 made four voyages between Singapore and Borneo. The impressions he gathered during these trips were to serve him variously and well, and to provide at least some of the inspiration for *Almayer's Folly*, *An Outcast of the Islands*, *Lord Jim*, 'The End of the Tether' (1902), *The Shadow Line*, and *The Rescue*. The important point here, as Mr Najder has observed, is that these trips on the *Vidar* gave Conrad his first genuine opportunity to see the East at close range, unconcealed by port buildings, hotels, offices, and colonial institutions. The *Vidar* penetrated inland, often steaming miles up the rivers of Borneo to deliver its various cargoes. Here, against the lush tropical background, the isolated trading posts must have impressed Conrad as foolish challenges to invincible and unseen forces, as pathetic proofs, were any needed, of human vanity. Here he met white men, Europeans, cut off from civilization, who sometimes became deranged in their exile.

It was while on one of his journeys up a river in Borneo that Conrad met the Eurasian Dutch trader Charles William Olmeijer, who had lived at his outpost for the past seventeen years. Like Conrad's Almayer, he was married to a woman of mixed caste by whom he had children and was constantly engaged in a struggle for power with a local chieftain named Abdulla. 'I [saw] him for the first time . . . from the bridge of a steamer moored to a rickety little wharf forty miles up, more or less, a Bornean river,' Conrad tells us in *A Personal Record*. Having tried and failed to get himself started as a writer of fiction with 'The Black Mate,' Conrad was seeking, more consciously this time, another subject. 'That morning, seeing the figure in pyjamas moving in the mist, I said to myself: "That's the man."' Olmeijer—of which Almayer is a phonetic English transcription—had come down (in his pyjamas) to the wharf to pick up from the *Vidar* his cargo, which on this trip consisted of a pony for one of his children. Conrad recalled that he did not want to look at his mail: 'I shall never forget that man afraid of his letters.' He adds: 'if I had not got to know Almayer pretty well it is almost certain there would never have been a line of mine in print.'

This final statement should not be taken too seriously. In fact Conrad never got to know the real Olmeijer at all well; and in any case, when someone is ready to write, as Conrad was by 1887–88, there will always be an Olmeijer to hand.

Why, one might ask, was it Borneo—rather than Singapore, or India, or Australia, or South Africa, or for that matter England—that drew him at last into the writing of fiction? What, in that Malay Archipelago, touched him into creative life? The answer is not easy; but there are clues. The time and the place were right, and the man was now watching out for 'material'. The Malayan scene plays an important role only in his early works. Conrad, the exile and wanderer without a home except for the British ensign over his head, would have been aware of the lack of almost any cultural background potential readers, British or otherwise, could have found to share with this first of his fictional communities. The subject and the setting provided a safe ground for fiction without risking discussion of matters with which English readers might have been better acquainted than he was himself. Indeed, he may have found himself hard pressed; Almayer and his trading post were a godsend. Conrad's potential readers, he knew, would have been more familiar with life in Greater Britain, its idioms and its fashions, than *he* was. Singapore, India, Australia, and South Africa, with their British connections, would be known to a dangerous number of English readers. But not the Malay Archipelago; not then, at any rate, before the fiction-writing days of Somerset Maugham and H. E. Bates. It was utterly and safely non-English.

Olmeijer and his surroundings were perfect for Conrad in other ways. The themes of moral and physical isolation, the dreariness of human life, the paralysis of human will, and the destructive potentiality of physical nature, especially in the face of that paralysis, accorded with Conrad's mood in the late eighties; he saw them *all* as subjects. And along came Almayer. And so it happened that his first novel would be set in Borneo, and that its central character would be isolated there.

In the story of these three decades we can see at least some of the origins of Conrad's characteristic vein as a writer of fiction. In all of his works—*all*, without exception—an individual or a small group of people find themselves in isolated circumstances, physically or spiritually, whether in Africa or the Far East or England, whether at sea or in a city or on an island. Life appears both fragile and cheap, easily lost and easily undervalued. Conrad's characters are almost all of them *strangers* in one way or another—foreigners, intruders, anomalies, exiles. No matter what they do or where they go, they remain psychologically isolated. The novelist drew from his terrifying ordeal by loneliness the knowledge that isolation—such as that of Decoud in *Nostromo*, for example—can make you mad. Isolation corrupts: it is one of Conrad's most famous themes. Men alone cannot be trusted. No other writer is so certain of this—so certain that human intercourse, society of some sort, is *required* to keep men both sane and good. It is a measure both of Conrad's solitariness as a boy and young man and of the pessimism about life which was one result of it. No one else argues so eloquently as Conrad does, indirectly though it may often be, how important it is for people to live together peaceably and honestly. It is the tragic fate of many of his protagonists to be unable to do so; the characters of *Victory* (1915) and those of *The Secret Agent*, one group on an island and the other in the heart of London, come to grief because they are unable to bridge that distance between human beings seen by Conrad as unavoidable.

When Conrad was thirty he declared that the quality he felt he most lacked was self-confidence. As a boy he had once broken in on the conversation of adults with the question, 'And what do you think of *me*?' The mature man was renowned among his contemporaries for a mercurial temperament, for 'nerves'. Throughout the rest of his life he was sometimes prostrated by depression so acute he was unable to lift a pen. And yet his work, gloomy as it is, is marked by a moral strength and sanity that demonstrate the power of his personality and his will in overcoming these potentially crippling debilities. The novels and stories Conrad wrote after *Almayer's Folly* continue to place his characters in harrowing spiritual and physical isolation. He finds more ways than any other writer to quarantine his people. Almayer, standing in his pyjamas alone on that Bornean quay, was just the beginning. Those of Conrad's characters who think too much in isolated circumstances—like Decoud, or Kurtz in 'Heart of Darkness' (1902), or a dozen other Conradian protagonists—go mad. Things do not bear much looking into, as Winnie Verloc discovers, to her horror, in *The Secret Agent*. For Conrad, the greatest danger of isolation is that it leads to thought, and thought is the enemy of mankind. Finally—Conrad believed that 'a novelist lives in his work. He stands there, the only reality in an invented world, among imaginary things, happenings, and people. Writing about them, he is only writing about himself.' Conrad understood how fiction grows out of life. He always found it almost impossible to revise his work because, as he told Garnett, 'I cannot meddle with what is within myself.' And while his life changed dramatically in its outward circumstances after the summer of 1889, when Conrad sat down in his London lodgings to write the first chapter of *Almayer's Folly*, the *inner* man *never* changed. Being, as he said, 'the only reality in an invented world,' the same hopes, fears, and memories got themselves translated again and again into his fiction.

As late as 1897, after explaining that up to that moment 'Most of my life has been spent between sky and water,' Conrad, then forty, wrote to a friend: 'I live so alone that often I fancy myself clinging stupidly to a derelict planet abandoned by its precious crew.' By this time he had published *Almayer's Folly*, *An Outcast of the Islands*, *The Nigger of the 'Narcissus'*, 'An Outpost of Progress', 'The Lagoon', and 'Karain', and was well launched on his new career; he had become the friend of John Galsworthy, Edward Garnett, T. Fisher Unwin, Henry James, Stephen Crane, R. B. Cunninghame Graham, William Blackwood, and A. T. Quiller-Couch, among others; and he had married. And yet he continued to live, as he put it, 'so alone' that it seemed as if he inhabited an empty planet. He remained imprisoned within himself. His life from an early age was a series of adaptations to odd circumstances that kept him perpetually off balance. In a very real sense, Conrad's discomposure was his passport to distinction.

Why, the critic Q. D. Leavis asked, does Conrad 'rub in so intolerably the inescapable isolation of every man?' Surely now we know. The little boy who wanted so badly to hear what the adults thought of *him* had grown up to become, in a phrase familiar to readers of *Lord Jim*, one of *them*. And still he was alone.

Willard Connely Memorial Lecture

LAMPEDUSA: THE GENESIS OF 'THE LEOPARD'

DAVID GILMOUR

Read 16 February 1989
John Grigg, FRSL, in the Chair

DURING his early life Giuseppe di Lampedusa gave a few scattered indications that he aspired to a literary career. As a timid and introverted child, he hid from his contemporaries and spent much of his time reading in the ancestral libraries of his parents' houses. As a youth he attempted to study literature at Rome University. And in his twenties he wrote three very long and curious articles—one of them called 'W. B. Yeats e il Risorgimento Irlandese'—for an obscure Genoese journal. But after that there was nothing. For the next twenty-eight years Lampedusa wrote nothing at all except for his letters, which are not particularly interesting and reveal scant literary talent. His letters to his fiancée were admittedly written as literary pieces in an ornate Proustian style. But he abandoned this affectation after his marriage and the rest of his correspondence with her, though still in French, is plain, matter-of-fact and banal.

The question I have most often been asked about Lampedusa is the most interesting one and also the most difficult to answer: why did someone of such immense talent wait until he was fifty-eight before writing a masterpiece? I have heard a number of theories, vaguely

Freudian in inspiration, attempting to explain both what had held him back for so long and what had then impelled him to begin. I don't think that on the whole these have been very helpful, and certainly they are not based on any known evidence. I think the real reasons for his 'writer's block' are to be found in his family, in his upbringing and in the various disappointments he experienced during a frustrating, sad and often pathetic life.

One of Lampedusa's chief handicaps was his family, both its past, which had left a depressing legacy of decline, and its present, in the shape of various living members. His father's family was very dull and did no work except for one uncle who was a diplomat. He used to boast that he was the first Lampedusa to work, and he was also the last. Although the family had lost most of its fortune through a divided inheritance and legal squabbling, it seems never to have occurred to the other Lampedusas that they should earn a living. Nor did they do much with their leisure except to go horse-racing; none of them was known to open a book.

It was bad luck that Lampedusa should have a father like Prince Giulio, a quarrelsome tyrant whose chief hobby was blackballing candidates for Palermo's most exclusive club. For various complicated legal reasons, Prince Giulio had inherited only two per cent of his grandfather's estate, and this embittered him so much that he spent most of his life quarrelling with his relations over money. He thought literature was an effeminate pastime and tried to discourage his son's enthusiasm for it. When Giuseppe asked to study literature at university, he refused. Like many fathers in southern Italy, Prince Giulio regarded a law degree as the ideal education for a gentleman, even if that gentleman had no intention of becoming a lawyer. And so his son studied law.

Giuseppe's mother Beatrice, who came from a more civilized family, was an intelligent and sophisticated woman. She encouraged her son's literary interests, taught him to speak French and later took him on tours of Europe. But unfortunately her influence on his life was even more harmful than his father's. Giuseppe was her only surviving child and she smothered him with affection, always treating him, even after his marriage, as if he was still a small boy. Even when he was doing military training during the First World War, she sent him a stream of letters—addressing him curiously in the feminine—urging him to go straight to bed if he thought he was catching a cold.

While she lived, Lampedusa was unable to detach himself from Beatrice's overpowering influence. When he decided to marry, at the age of thirty-five, he was terrified by his mother's reaction and even pretended—after the wedding—than he was still only engaged. The marriage had taken place in Latvia where his wife Alessandra—half-Balt and half-Italian—had an estate, and from there Giuseppe sent his mother long letters imploring her blessing. Although she eventually complied, she was determined to make life impossible for the new couple when they settled in Palermo. Alessandra was also a formidable woman but Beatrice's hold over her son was so strong that there was little doubt about the outcome of the contest. A year after their marriage, Alessandra returned to Latvia while Lampedusa stayed with his mother in Sicily. They did not live together again for another eleven years when both of them were homeless: near the end of the Second World War Alessandra's Baltic estate was taken over by the Russians and Giuseppe's Palermo palace was bombed by the Americans.

Towards the end of his life Lampedusa wrote a short note in praise of British public schools in which he argued that 'separation from the family and a life with contemporaries eradicates that type of 'mamma's boy' so perniciously frequent the more one travels to the south [of Europe]; compulsory sports in the open air in any weather prevent timidity and physical fear and train one for rapid decisions and teamwork.' It was surely the memory of his own upbringing which led Lampedusa to write like that. Because he was timid, he was in many ways a 'mamma's boy', and he was quite incapable of making decisions. It is difficult to imagine Lampedusa writing *The Leopard* while his mother was still alive; he did not mind libelling Sicily and infuriating the Sicilians, but he would have been terrified of his mother's disapproval. Proust had been unable to begin work on his massive novel until after his mother's death, and likewise Beatrice's death in 1946 removed one of the obstacles preventing her son from writing.·

But there were other obstacles. After Giuseppe's death, his cousin Lucio Piccolo was asked why Lampedusa had not begun writing until so near the end of his life. Piccolo, who was a poet, replied: 'We Sicilians are so afraid of being badly judged on the mainland that we prefer to keep silent.' The remark is of course an exaggeration —Verga, Pirandello and many other Sicilian writers showed no such reticence—but it does contain an element of truth in the case of

Lampedusa. He was a very shy man, he hated social life and, besides, he was entirely unambitious. Like many Sicilians, he had little desire to compete in the outside world and even as a child he had been uncompetitive both at school and at games.

He was also, by nature, lazy, particularly as a young man. A letter written to Alessandra before their marriage describes a typical day of his life in Palermo: most of it was occupied by eating or chatting at his club, and much of the rest of his time was spent ambling between cafes, bookshops and his library. His life contained certain events—a year's imprisonment in the First World War, long journeys through Europe, marriage and its problems, and two years as President of the Sicilian Red Cross after the Second World War—but little else until the final three years. As a child he discovered that he liked solitude and reading books and his tastes did not change when he became an adult. He set himself no task in life except, perhaps, to read every book he could lay his hands on, even if this meant learning new languages. He read very widely in English, French, Italian and German, and when he had exhausted their literatures near the end of his life, he turned to Russian and Spanish.

Lampedusa's detachment from contemporary events is illustrated by his attitude to fascism. He hated the Italian liberals for historic reasons, for their neglect of Sicily since Unification, and hoped for a short time that Mussolini might have more to offer the south. His optimism did not last. He disliked the demagoguery and the endless military parades, and he enjoyed ridiculing the regime in private. Yet he also thought that fascism was what the Italians needed and deserved, and he was therefore not prepared to oppose it. The fact is that he did not really care about contemporary politics. He was more interested in comparing the merits of Cromwell and Charles II, which he could do by himself in his library, than in discussing the future of fascism or democracy in Italy.

I have suggested that his family, upbringing and character all hindered Lampedusa's development as a writer. Another factor, which in the end paradoxically helped in the creation of *The Leopard* itself, was the history and decline of his family. He would have liked to have been a wealthy enlightened prince of the eighteenth century, using his education both for his scholarly interests and for the well-being of his estates. Instead he was an impoverished aristocrat living a most unprincely existence in Palermo; in the 1930s he even had to let half of his palace to the municipal gas board. Much of his time was spent, uselessly, trying to sort out the inheritance of his great-grandfather, who had died of cholera in Florence without making a will. This involved endless meetings with his second cousins whom he described in English in a letter to Alessandra as 'a remarkable assembly of people, one-third fools, one-third lunatics, and the rest of them rascals'.

The Sicilian aristocracy had lost its political power before Lampedusa's birth, and its prosperity and social influence had been declining rapidly since his childhood. He was well aware that as a prince he had no proper function in Sicily. Yet he could not escape into anonymity, at least before the Second World War. He was still expected to play a social role, to act as an emblem of a vanishing world, even if this meant taking part in events such as fancy-dress balls which he hated. So he escaped abroad, primarily to England where his uncle was ambassador, and there he did not have to play a role, except occasionally at embassy functions in the evenings. London, he recalled once, was the only city where one could find the satisfaction of 'disappearing, of losing oneself in an ocean, of not being anyone'.

Yet he could not escape for long. Palermo and Beatrice always called him back. Even his marriage did not loosen his bonds to a city which annoyed him, to a mother who dominated him, and to a family almost submerged by litigation and financial problems. When he was forced to take sides in the struggle between his mother and his wife, he preferred Beatrice and Palermo to Alessandra and the Baltic.

One of the most revealing characters in *The Leopard* is Giovanni, described as 'the most loved, the most difficult' of Don Fabrizio's sons. Giovanni does not actually appear in the novel because he has already run away to London, preferring a modest life as a clerk in a coal depot to a pampered and fettered existence in the ease of Palermo. As we have seen, Lampedusa was too timid, too indolent and too tied to his mother to do the same thing. Yet Giovanni is in some ways the person Lampedusa would have liked to have been. If he had broken away like Giovanni, his literary career would surely have begun earlier, but then he would have been a very different writer and *The Leopard* would never have been written. Because even though those Sicilian fetters prevented Lampedusa from writing for so long, the experience of them enabled him in the end to write a masterpiece. One of the reasons he wrote so well about his island is that he—almost uniquely among Sicilian writers of his and the two previous generations—stayed there and wrote about the place as he saw it and not with the sentimental eyes of an exile in the north.

Two of the saddest events in his life were the loss of his two childhood homes, the country house of his mother's family at Santa Margherita di Belice and the palace of his father's family in Palermo. Santa Margherita, a beautiful place which Lampedusa described and magnified as Donnafugata in *The Leopard*, was sold to pay the debts of his maternal uncle, an eccentric character who endeavoured to combine the role of a flamboyant prince with his career as a socialist deputy. Lampedusa was badly affected by its loss, but the destruction of his own palace in Palermo hit him even harder. When he had seen the results of the bombing he walked to a friend's house and stayed there for three days, too stunned to say anything except to repeat over and over again that his home had been wrecked.

Lampedusa often brooded over the history of his family and the disappearance of its property. After one visit to the former ancestral estates at Palma di Montechiaro, he was profoundly moved and noted in his diary that he felt 'orphaned and melancholic'. His wife Alessandra realised how strongly he had been affected by the loss and encouraged him to write about those places in order to mitigate his depression and to 'neutralize his nostalgia'. Eventually she was successful. Lampedusa's memories of the lost palaces and his wife's urgings that he should evoke them on paper were important factors in his decision to write.

The Tomasi di Lampedusa family had a long ancestry which has traditionally been traced back to the early Byzantine emperors. Even if the true lineage is in fact less exotic, Lampedusa was still aware that he was the ultimate descendant of an ancient noble line whose economic and physical extinction culminated in himself. The consciousness of his family's decadence often depressed him and increasingly, towards the end of his life, he felt the need to record something of the process which had caused it. In *The Leopard* he described Don Fabrizio 'watching the ruins of his own class and his own inheritance without even making, still less wanting to make, any move towards saving it.' Yet both the author and his protagonist did care about that inheritance, not because of what it brought in material benefits but because of what it represented in the form of tradition and family history. The decadence of the Lampedusas was resented by Giuseppe because it consigned his family to history. On his deathbed Don Fabrizio reflects that 'the significance of a noble family lies entirely in its traditions, that is in its vital memories; and he was the last to have any unusual memories, anything different from other families'. Lampedusa also had those memories, and it was his need to preserve them, before they disappeared for ever, that compelled him to start writing.

Giuseppe di Lampedusa did not see the decline of his family simply as an isolated regression, of importance only to himself and his relations. It was an illustration of the decline of a ruling class which had ruled Sicily—on the whole very badly—ever since the Normans conquered the island in the eleventh century. The history of his family was inseparable from the history of Sicily, and both had been going downhill, in seemingly irreversible decline, for several generations. Moreover, the most important political event of recent times, Unification, had not halted that decline in the south of Italy. Lampedusa wanted to discuss the history of Sicily from the times of its earliest conquerors, but decided to concentrate on the period of the Risorgimento, to base his story around an allegedly heroic national movement and to examine what had gone wrong. *The Leopard* thus begins in 1860, the year of Garibaldi's invasion of Sicily, and ends fifty years later, shortly before the First World War. The sterility and decay of the final chapter is a symbol of the failure of the Italian liberals—after half a century of government—to regenerate Sicily.

Lampedusa was consistently derogatory about his own island and both his writings and his conversation were permeated with sarcasm about his fellow-countrymen. He used to refer to Sicily as '*questo* backwater' and compare it to Peru, which he had never visited and knew little about. The island's provincialism constantly astonished him and he advised his friends to read Conrad as an antidote to the intolerable stagnation of life in Palermo. Yet he admitted that few Sicilians would be able to understand Conrad, even in translation. 'A lady whom we all know,' he once recounted, 'was returning to Palermo after an absence of only two days. On reaching Porta Felice she made the sign of the cross and thanked the Lord for allowing her to see her native city once more . . . How is it possible that this lady could ever be interested in Conrad, who for twenty years wandered around the Pacific, or Kipling, who spent half his time between London and India?'

The Leopard, the short story 'Lighea' and the last thing Lampedusa wrote—the opening chapter of a novel he was planning to call *The Blind Kittens*—are all full of references to alleged Sicilian defects:

their vanity, their idleness, their lack of intelligence which is disguised by their 'quick wits', their 'terrifying insularity of mind', their 'impermeability to anything new'. The protagonist of 'Lighea', a strongly autobiographical character, refers to the Sicilians as 'donkeys'. Yet even he, a great classical scholar, is a provincial, described as 'one of those Sicilians who consider the Ligurian Riviera . . . a kind of Iceland'.

Occasionally one of Lampedusa's characters is portrayed as a decent and honest person in order to emphasize the deficiencies of the others. For example, in describing someone in *The Blind Kittens* as 'a person of sensitive feelings', Lampedusa felt compelled to remind us that this was 'a human species very rare in Sicily'. And even if some individuals were exempted from his relentless criticism, the author showed no such leniency to social classes. *The Leopard* is often rather simplistically regarded as a polemic against the bourgeoisie, and indeed, Lampedusa, who admired the middle classes in Britain and France, did castigate the 'tenacious greed and avarice' of their Sicilian counterparts whom he regarded as little better than prototype *mafiosi*. Yet the peasant class is also subjected to some robust terminology—its 'men of honour' dismissed as 'violent imbeciles capable of any carnage', and so is the aristocracy; in *The Blind Kittens* the nobles in their club are frivolous and ineffective with 'frothy and infantile imaginations'. In spite of class differences Lampedusa believed it possible to identify a collective Sicilian mentality and in *The Leopard* he gave Don Fabrizio the opportunity to explain it to the bemused Piedmontese official:

> In Sicily it doesn't matter about doing things well or badly; the sin which we Sicilians never forgive is simply that of 'doing' at all . . . Sleep, my dear Chevalley, sleep, that is what Sicilians want, and they will always hate anyone who tries to wake them, even in order to bring them the most wonderful of gifts . . . your only mistake was saying 'the Sicilians must want to improve' . . . the Sicilians never want to improve for the simple reason that they think themselves perfect; their vanity is stronger than their misery.

Many of the Italian critics who reacted strongly against this view of Sicily missed one important point: the anti-Sicilian polemic which Lampedusa was accused of could only have been written by someone who loved Sicily as well as hated it, by someone who still loved what he believed to be irredeemable. He saw the island as a place of contrasts and extremes—a country 'in which the inferno round Randazzo is a few miles from the beauty of Taormina bay'. The critics noticed the hatred and disgust but not the love for that 'archaic and aromatic countryside' which the Greek and Phoenician colonists had encountered. The island's essence is beautifully evoked in 'Lighea' when Lampedusa describes

> 'eternal Sicily, nature's Sicily'; 'the scent of rosemary on the Nèbrodi hills, the taste of Melilli honey, the waving corn seen from Etna on a windy day in May . . . the solitudes around Syracuse, the gusts of scent from orange and lemon groves pouring over Palermo . . . during some sunsets in June . . . the enchantment of certain summer nights within sight of Castellamare bay, when stars are mirrored in the sleeping sea and the spirit of anyone lying back amid the lentisks is lost in a vortex of sky, while the body is tense and alert, fearing the approach of demons.'

Lampedusa saw Sicily as an Arcadia ruined over 'twenty-five centuries' of mismanagement and neglect, its grandeur corrupted by history but still visible in decay. And he wanted his work to convey the effect of this historical legacy on Sicily. As Don Fabrizio explains to the Piedmontese official who believed that Italian unity would bring progress and enlightenment to Sicily,

> We are old Chevalley, very old. For over twenty-five centuries we've been bearing the weight of superb and heterogeneous civilizations, all from outside, none made by ourselves, none that we could call our own. We're as white as you are, Chevalley, and as the Queen of England; and yet for two thousand years we've been a colony. I don't say that in complaint; it's our fault. But even so we're worn out and exhausted . . . You talked to me a short while ago about a young Sicily sighting the marvels of the modern world; for my part I see instead a centenarian being dragged in a bath-chair round the Great Exhibition in London, understanding nothing and caring about nothing . . .

Lampedusa was writing nearly a hundred years after Garibaldi's conquest of Sicily. He had read a lot about the era of the Risorgimento, about the triumphs of Unification, about the new age of Liberty and Progress it was supposed to bring the people of the south. He lived in a country in which the achievements of national unity are commemorated everywhere. How many Italian towns do not have a

Via Cavour, a Piazza Garibaldi or a Corso Vittorio Emanuele? Yet to Lampedusa the achievement was essentially a myth, its attainment a fraud on the Italian people. And in his writing he was eager to demonstrate why this was so.

The Leopard contains numerous jibes and criticisms of the Risorgimento, but the most memorable passage is a soliloquy of Don Fabrizio at Donnafugata when he recalls the deceptions of the plebiscite, the rigged vote which produced figures showing that 99.8 per cent of Sicilian voters had supported unity. To Don Fabrizio, the lying of the plebiscite killed the people's faith in the new regime. To Lampedusa it demonstrated the real nature of Piedmontese power and he was unable to resist adding his own postscript to Fabrizio's reflections:

> Don Fabrizio could not have known it then, but a great deal of the slackness and acquiescence for which the people of the south were to be criticized during the following decades, was due to the stupid annulment of the first expression of liberty ever offered them.

Although his need to record past memories and his desire to explain the decline of both his family and his island are the underlying reasons behind Lampedusa's decision to write, he still needed something else, an additional incentive, to make him sit down and pick up his pen. In 1953–4 two important events took place. Encouraged by his wife, he decided to give informal literature lessons in his house to a small group of friends. He began enthusiastically, discarding his habitual laziness, and in less than a year he had written a thousand pages covering the entire period of English literature from Bede to Graham Greene. When he had finished he turned to French writers and then to Goethe. He enjoyed the project because it gave him an excuse to re-read his favourite authors and to convey his enjoyment and understanding of literature to others. Besides, it gave him the opportunity to think about novel-writing and to wonder whether it was really as difficult as he had previously thought.

The second event provided the crucial spur. In 1954 his cousin Lucio Piccolo asked Lampedusa to accompany him to a major conference in northern Italy where he was to receive a prize for his poetry. Lucio was as learned as Lampedusa and a talented eccentric in many fields: a musician who played Wagner by ear and spent many years composing an unfinished Magnificat, he had once corresponded with W. B. Yeats about different sorts of elves, comparing Irish goblins with their Sicilian equivalents. The literary rapport between Lucio and Giuseppe was so close that neither of them had bothered to look for other intellectual friends. For more than thirty years they played esoteric literary games, writing sketches and verses and then ruthlessly criticizing each other's efforts. Like Lampedusa, Lucio felt no great need to broadcast his talents until one day in 1954 when he decided to publish his poems and duly won a prize.

Lampedusa was not greatly impressed by the literary conference. He was sceptical about the eminent writers he saw strutting self-importantly around, and felt—rightly as it turned out—that he could write prose as well as any of them. Moreover, the sight of Lucio winning a prize at last aroused some feeling of competitiveness. After the conference he returned to Sicily and began work. As he later explained in a letter to a friend, 'Being mathematically certain that I was no more of a fool [than Lucio], I sat down and wrote a novel.'

And so, of course, he did. He began slowly and diffidently, telling his wife and uncle that he was scribbling away for his own amusement. Yet once he had taken the decision to start, he committed himself to his writing. Spurred on by the realization that his health was not good, he worked almost every day for the last thirty months of his life. In that time, besides his teaching, he wrote three drafts of *The Leopard*, two short stories, an autobiography of his childhood and the beginning of another novel.

Before he had begun to write, Giuseppe di Lampedusa was sometimes overcome by a sense of futility, by the consciousness of his family's decline, and by the realization that he had wasted his life. But that late discovery of a true vocation changed everything; it gave him a purpose in living and therefore a reason to delay dying. He became obsessed by his work and wanted to write more and more. And he would have done so if lung cancer had not overtaken him so shortly after he had at last realised what he could contribute to literature. The tragedy of Lampedusa was the coincidence of his physical decadence with his brief period of artistic activity.